**Illustrator**
Howard Chaney

**Editor**
Walter Kelly, M.A.

**Editorial Project Manager**
Ina Massler Levin, M.A.

**Editor-in-Chief**
Sharon Coan, M.S. Ed.

**Creative Director**
Elayne Roberts

**Associate Designer**
Denise Bauer

**Cover Artist**
Elayne Roberts

**Product Manager**
Phil Garcia

**Imaging**
Hillary Merriman

**Publisher**
Mary D. Smith, M.S. Ed.

# Middle School Study S[...]

D1495815

**Author**

*John Ernst*

***Teacher Created Resources, Inc.***
6421 Industry Way
Westminster, CA 92683
www.teachercreated.com

**ISBN: 978-1-55734-194-5**

*©1996 Teacher Created Resources, Inc.*
Reprinted, 2010
Made in U.SA.

# Table of Contents

# To the Teacher

Kudos to you and the wonderful job you do as a teacher. You work hard every day to help your students learn the knowledge and develop the skills that will prepare them for their adult lives. As you know, however, you cannot always be there for your students. Much of their time studying and learning is spent on their own. Therefore, it is important that students know how to study effectively, and it helps a great deal if they are organized. A few study strategies, along with proper organization, can instill in each student a sense of confidence and control.

This book was designed to help students develop the study skills and organizational skills which can help them to become independent, self-sufficient learners. It can be used individually by a student or as a resource for a teacher for group or individual instruction.

There are three main parts to this book. **Part One: Getting It Together** is about getting organized. It includes tips on things like how to organize papers, how to keep track of homework, and how to create a daily schedule. **Part Two: What's My Grade?** is about grades and how to keep track of grade averages. **In Part Three: Learning to Learn**, there are several study strategies which can help students improve their productivity when studying. Each part is organized into chapters, and each chapter focuses on a different idea.

Feel free to modify the strategies presented in this book in order to meet your needs or the needs of your students. You may want to encourage your students to develop their own study techniques based on the strategies that work best for them, given their individual learning styles. You may also want to suggest specific strategies to individual students which may help them cope with certain problems related to learning ability.

The student pages in this book are reproducible. From these pages you can create a booklet for each student. Alternatively, you can create smaller packets of pages from certain chapters, and present students with successive packets. You may ask that your students keep these pages in a binder or folder for reference.

Certainly, nothing can replace the teacher as a facilitator of meaningful learning. Yet, simple, effective study strategies do have their place among the abundance of resources students and teachers can rely on to enhance learning. It is hoped that you and your students will find the ideas presented in this book helpful.

# To the Student

This study skills book was created for students like you. It was written with these three things in mind: (1) students want to do well in school; (2) students who consistently do well in school practice good study habits and are well organized; and (3) study skills and organizational skills do not come naturally to most people—they must be learned.

With the study strategies and organizational strategies in this book, you can learn the skills and develop the habits that will help you succeed in school. And good study skills and organizational skills do even more—they actually help make school easier because they put you in control. When it comes to a test, you will be totally ready. And when it is time to turn in homework, you will know just where to find your assignments. All in all, good study skills and organizational skills can help you to get more done in less time, and that means less time on homework with better results!

There are three main parts to this book. **Part One: Getting It Together** is about getting organized. In this first part, you will find tips on things such as how to organize your papers, how to keep track of homework, and how to manage your time. **Part Two: What's My Grade?** is about grades and how to keep track of what your grade is in each class. **In Part Three: Learning to Learn**, you will find several study strategies which can help you become an expert studier. Each part is organized into chapters, and each chapter focuses on a different idea.

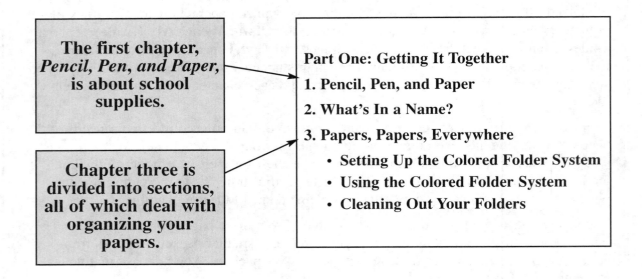

**The first chapter, *Pencil, Pen, and Paper,* is about school supplies.**

**Chapter three is divided into sections, all of which deal with organizing your papers.**

**Part One: Getting It Together**

**1. Pencil, Pen, and Paper**

**2. What's In a Name?**

**3. Papers, Papers, Everywhere**

- **Setting Up the Colored Folder System**
- **Using the Colored Folder System**
- **Cleaning Out Your Folders**

There are several forms from which you may make copies in the appendix at the back of this book. Be sure not to write on the originals, since you will want to have new forms for future classes. The appendix begins on page 131.

Before you start reading, glance through the book and take a look at the table of contents. Then either read straight through and choose the sections that interest you most. If something is unclear, ask a parent, another student, or a teacher for help. Use the ideas you like, and feel free to change an idea to meet your needs. You might even come up with a few ideas of your own. If you find something that works well, share it with a friend or your teacher.

# Part One: Getting It Together

Part One of this book is designed to help students get organized. Actually, getting organized is easy. The real challenge for many students is to *stay* organized. The strategies presented in the chapters that follow can help students to develop consistent and reliable methods of organizing their materials, their papers, and their time.

## Part One

Chapter 1: **Pencil, Pen, and Paper** is all about supplies. Students can keep track of the supplies they need with the Supplies Update List.

Chapter 2: **What's in a Name?** is about how to label papers. This fundamental procedure can save time and energy for the student and the teacher.

Chapter 3: **Papers, Papers, Everywhere** deals with keeping track of papers. Here, a folder system and a binder system are presented.

Chapter 4: **Homework Helpers** is about how to manage homework with a homework list, an assignment sheet, or an assignment notebook.

Chapter 5: **Getting Set Up for Class** shows students a proactive approach to getting their materials set up at the beginning of class.

Chapter 6: **Managing Your Time** introduces the concept of time management, emphasizes the importance of daily study sessions, and outlines the use of a daily schedule and a monthly calendar.

Chapter 7: **Being the Messenger** introduces a system whereby parents and students work as a team to be sure that important papers get home and back to school.

Chapter 8: **A Place to Study** illustrates how to set up a great work station at home and emphasizes the need for a quiet, well-lit place to study.

Depending on the needs of your students, you may want to go through the strategies in order, or you may want to skip around. If you are incorporating study skills lessons into your academic classes, you may wish to introduce one strategy per week. To help your students develop these strategies into habits, they will need frequent reminders, review, and reinforcement, especially during the time immediately following the introduction of a strategy.

What is important, however, is that the methods your students use are uniform and consistent. You may want to request that all students in your classes use identical methods of organization. In cases where students are shared among several teachers, it is suggested that the teachers agree on and use uniform methods of organization.

# Pencil, Pen, and Paper

Too often, students are hindered in their progress because they do not have the supplies they need. They also suffer embarrassment when they have to admit that they are unprepared or when they have to borrow supplies from other students. This can lead to negative feelings about school and self. Such problems can be avoided if students develop a system of supply management. Such a system can be as easy as keeping a grocery list on the refrigerator.

This chapter is designed to help students keep track of their school supplies. At the beginning of the year, students can use the Class Supply List and the Supply Master List to list the supplies they will need to start the school year. Students can use the Supply Update List to list the supplies they need during the year. These forms can be found in the appendix. Examples of how to use these forms appear on the following pages. This chapter also includes information on how to take care of textbooks and instructions on how to cover a textbook.

## ─── Suggested Strategies and Activities ───

- At the beginning of the school year, have your students use the Class Supply List to list the supplies they will need for each of their classes. This form will not be needed if your students are given a comprehensive list of supplies they will need for all their classes.

- Have your students use the Supply Master List to compile a comprehensive list of the supplies they will need for all their classes. Ask them to include things they will need for their own use that were not suggested by their teachers, such as a book bag or computer floppy disks.

- Ask students to keep a copy of their Supply Update List in their home folder. (A home folder is a folder that the students take to every class and then home. The home folder is explained on pages 36 and 37.) When you assign your students work that involves special materials, such as poster board, ask them to list those materials on their Supply Update List.

- Educate the parents of your students about the use of the Supply Update List. Ask the parents to plan regular trips to the store for school supplies with the Supply Update List.

- As a class activity, have your students inventory their supplies at the end of each quarter.

- Ask your students to keep their receipts from the purchase of supplies. As a class activity, compile a list of supplies and their average costs.

- Students who have the supplies they need are often the target of solicitation by other students who do not. Have a policy which discourages borrowing and encourages students to get their own supplies. For example, no student may borrow paper from another student unless he/she has paid back what was previously borrowed. Ask students to list the material being borrowed on their Supplies Update List.

- Many students do not know how to cover their books properly. Have your students bring in paper grocery bags and cover textbooks as a class.

# Pencil, Pen, and Paper *(cont.)*

Walk into any store, office, or bank and you will see that the people working there have a need for supplies such as pens, note pads, paper clips, and tape. If it is a successful business, they will have plenty of the supplies they need on hand. A student's work requires a constant flow of supplies, just like a business. This chapter will show you how to keep track of the supplies you need for school. Follow the steps below. All forms mentioned below can be found in the appendix, which begins on page 131.

1. Check with each one of your teachers at the beginning of the year for a supply list. If you do not receive a supply list from a teacher, use the Class Supply List form to list the supplies you will need for that class. Take a look at the example below.

2. Use the Supply Master List form to make a list of all the supplies you will need to start the year. Take a look at the example on the next page.

3. Take the Supply Master List form with you to buy your supplies. This might take several trips to one or more stores.

4. Check your supplies at the end of each grading period or sooner. Use the Supply Update List form to list the things you need. Take a look at the example on the next page. Make regular trips to the store with this form.

Here is an example of how to use the Class Supply List. The supplies on your list might be different. You can see the entire form in the appendix on page 131.

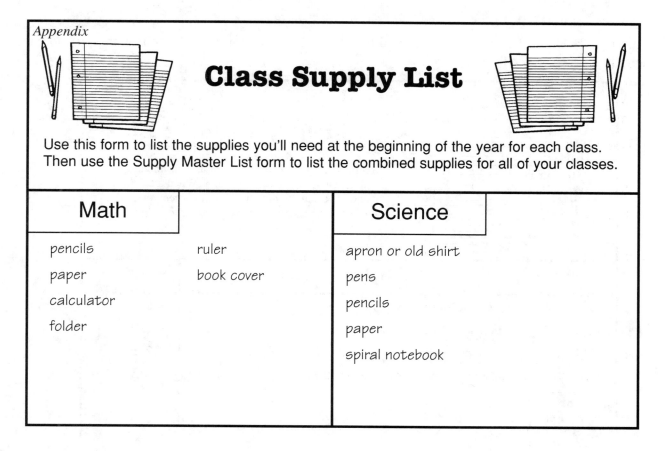

*Appendix*

# Class Supply List

Use this form to list the supplies you'll need at the beginning of the year for each class. Then use the Supply Master List form to list the combined supplies for all of your classes.

| Math | | Science | |
|---|---|---|---|
| pencils | ruler | apron or old shirt | |
| paper | book cover | pens | |
| calculator | | pencils | |
| folder | | paper | |
| | | spiral notebook | |

# Pencil, Pen, and Paper *(cont.)*

Now take a look at the Supply Master List. You will find two of these forms in the appendix; one has supply types listed for you.

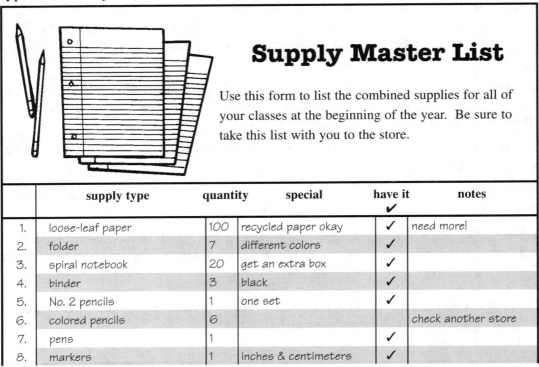

## Supply Master List

Use this form to list the combined supplies for all of your classes at the beginning of the year. Be sure to take this list with you to the store.

|     | supply type | quantity | special | have it ✔ | notes |
|-----|-------------|----------|---------|-----------|-------|
| 1.  | loose-leaf paper | 100 | recycled paper okay | ✓ | need more! |
| 2.  | folder | 7 | different colors | ✓ | |
| 3.  | spiral notebook | 20 | get an extra box | ✓ | |
| 4.  | binder | 3 | black | ✓ | |
| 5.  | No. 2 pencils | 1 | one set | ✓ | |
| 6.  | colored pencils | 6 | | | check another store |
| 7.  | pens | 1 | | ✓ | |
| 8.  | markers | 1 | inches & centimeters | ✓ | |

Use the Supply Update List to list things you need during the school year. Keep it with you and check it each night.

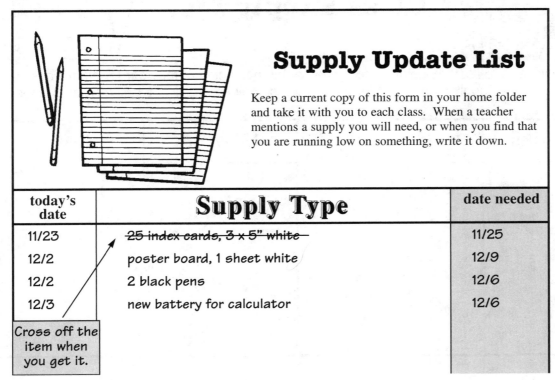

## Supply Update List

Keep a current copy of this form in your home folder and take it with you to each class. When a teacher mentions a supply you will need, or when you find that you are running low on something, write it down.

| today's date | Supply Type | date needed |
|--------------|-------------|-------------|
| 11/23 | ~~25 index cards, 3 x 5" white~~ | 11/25 |
| 12/2 | poster board, 1 sheet white | 12/9 |
| 12/2 | 2 black pens | 12/6 |
| 12/3 | new battery for calculator | 12/6 |

Cross off the item when you get it.

# **Pencil, Pen, and Paper** *(cont.)*

## Other Tips About Supplies

✔ Keep a copy of your Supplies Update List in your home folder. Home folders are explained on page 16.

✔ Keep a folder full of loose-leaf paper in your locker or desk. Label the folder "paper supply."

✔ Keep an extra box of pencils and an extra box of pens in your locker. You can never have too many pens and pencils.

✔ Replace old folders, book bags, and pencil cases before they fall apart, causing you to lose supplies and assignments.

✔ Buy good quality materials that will last.

✔ Buy your supplies at a discount warehouse or big office supply store. Prices will be lower, and the selection will be greater.

✔ Supplies can be expensive. Work out a budget with your parents for supplies to begin the year and supplies for throughout the year.

✔ Do not let other students rely on you for their supplies. Lend supplies only to those students who pay you back.

## Taking Care of Textbooks

Textbooks are meant to last because they are very expensive to replace. Some schools require students to pay for unusual damage done to their textbooks. You can help your school and your family by taking good care of your books. To help keep your textbooks in good shape, follow the guidelines below.

1. Always have a cover on each of your textbooks. Avoid taping the cover to the inside or outside of the book. Directions for covering textbooks are on the next page.

2. If you decorate your book cover, remove it from the book first. Permanent markers can bleed through the cover, and ballpoint pens can leave indentations on the book's hard cover.

3. Avoid writing in the book. Also, do not use the book as something to bear down on when writing because this can leave indentations on the book's hard cover or on the pages.

4. Do not keep papers inside the textbook. This can damage the binding, which is the most important part of the book.

5. When you are first issued a textbook, be sure to check it over carefully. Let your teacher know if you find any damage, such as torn pages or writing.

6. Be sure your book is completely labeled on the inside, with your name and your school's name. If it is not, let your teacher know.

7. Most books have an identification number on the inside of the hardcover. Write down the identification numbers of your textbooks. If your books are lost or stolen, you will have a better chance of finding them if you know the identification numbers.

8. Because your textbooks are valuable, you should not leave them unattended in places where they might be stolen.

# **Pencil, Pen, and Paper** *(cont.)*

**How to Cover Your Book**

1. The cover should be at least 6" (15 cm) wider than the book, and about 4" (10 cm) greater in length.  Cut it down to size if it is too big.

2. The side of the cover you wish to show on your book should be faced down.

3. Fold the top and bottom edges so that the length of the cover is slightly greater than the length of the book.

4. Center the book over the cover and fold both side edges over the book's hard cover, creating a sleeve on each end.  Slip one end of the hard cover into the sleeve and tape it on the top and bottom.  Be sure not to tape it to the book's hard cover.

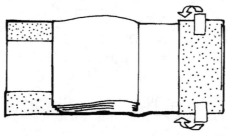

5. Slip the other end of the hard cover into the other sleeve.  Before you tape it, close the book all the way.  This is important because if you tape the sleeve while the book is open flat, the cover will be too short.  If done correctly, your book cover can be easily removed from the book by removing one sleeve at a time.

6. Remove the book cover from the book.  Label the cover with the name of the class, your name, the school, and your teacher's name.  Also, put the name of the class on the spine.

# What's in a Name

This chapter is devoted to helping students get in the habit of labeling their assignments. Assignments that are turned in without a proper label can cause an enormous amount of frustration for both teachers and students. For the teacher, it invariably means additional time spent figuring out what the assignment is and who it belongs to. For the student, it often means lost assignments (that would have been returned if properly labeled) or lower marks on assignments, both of which can lead to lower grades. Such frustration can be avoided. With practice, students can develop the habit of labeling their assignments, as well as their personal belongings.

There are many things you can do to help your students develop good labeling habits. First, be sure to make your expectations clear to your students about what information they should include in their labels and what format they should use. Present your instructions orally and visually, and give students a chance to practice. Second, agree on a uniform format for labels with other teachers who also teach your students. Students should be able to adapt to small variations in label format between teachers, but overall consistency will help them to develop good labeling habits.

In the following pages, a label is presented as having two parts—a heading and a title. The heading consists of the student's name, the date, and the subject. The title is the name of the assignment. In the format presented, the heading is located in the upper right corner of the paper, and the title is located on the first line. You may wish to customize the information in the label, as well as the format, in order to meet your needs.

## Suggested Strategies and Activities

- At the beginning of the year, present your students with a standard format for labeling their assignments. Make it clear what information you want in the label and where you want it to appear on the paper. Practice using this label with your students. An activity for doing this is provided on page 13.

- In your classroom, display an enlarged example of how you would like assignments to be labeled.

- At the beginning of an assignment, remind your students to label their papers. Repeat the title of the assignment several times, and write it on the chalkboard.

- Before collecting an assignment, ask your students to check a neighbor's paper for a complete and accurate label.

- Upon collecting an assignment, ask a student to look through the stack of papers and check for complete and accurate labels. Ask that student to set aside those papers that are labeled incorrectly. Return those papers to their owners for correction.

- In the case of an unusual assignment, such as a poster project or a clay model, be sure to include labeling instructions.

# What's In a Name? *(cont.)*

Thoroughly labeling your papers and projects can really help you to get organized. It is one of the best habits you can get into with your work. Labeling involves two things: (1) giving the assignment a **title** and (2) creating a **heading.**

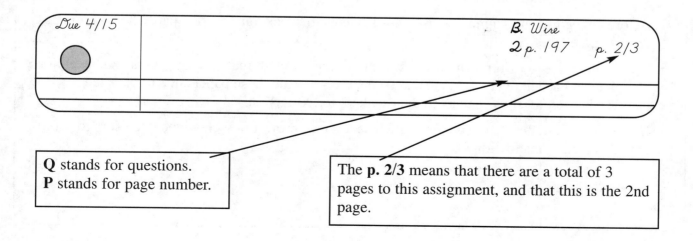

The **title** tells the reader what the assignment is. The **heading** gives the reader important information such as your name, the date, and the class. You might add more information, such as your teacher's name, the day of the week (T for Tuesday), and the due date (the date that the assignment is to be turned in).

Where you put this information on the page is called the **format.** In the format above, the heading is in the upper right corner, the title is on the first line, and a due date has been added in the upper left corner.

If the assignment requires more than one page, be sure to label the additional pages. Less information is needed on additional pages, and you can abbreviate. Take a look at the example below.

**Q** stands for questions.
**P** stands for page number.

The **p. 2/3** means that there are a total of 3 pages to this assignment, and that this is the 2nd page.

# What's In a Name? *(cont.)*

There are many ways to format your label.  Check with each teacher about what information each would like to see in a label and what format each would prefer.

## Exercise: Labeling Practice

Label the page below with information from your teacher.  Use the format that your teacher prefers.

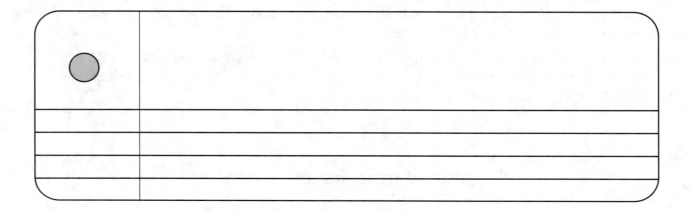

## Other Labeling Tips

✔ The most important part of your label is your name.  Even if you are in a rush, be sure to put your name on your assignment.

✔ Avoid using initials in the heading on the first page; write out your first and last name.

✔ Label your book covers on the front and the spine.

✔ Label the things you take to school, such as your lunch, book bag, purse, wallet, calculator, musical instrument, etc.

✔ Projects should also be clearly labeled with a heading on the front and back.

✔ When there is more than one page to your assignment, staple the papers together.

✔ Grading papers that are without a title and a name can be very frustrating.  Many teachers will not grade papers that lack complete labels.

✔ Getting into the habit of putting a complete label on all of your work and your belongings will save you much time and trouble.

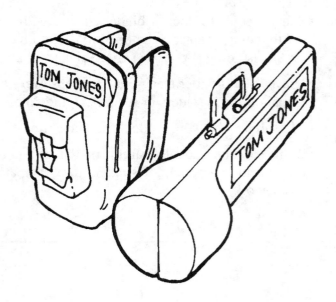

# Papers, Papers, Everywhere!

Until modern technology replaces the student notebook with a floppy disk, papers will continue to be an integral part of the school environment. Many students are unsuccessful in school because they have difficulty functioning within this perpetual paper environment. These students could greatly benefit from training in a system for organizing their papers.

There are many effective ways for students to organize their papers. This chapter presents two basic methods: using folders, and using a binder. In both cases, it is assumed that the student attends several different academic classes. Guidelines are also given for cleaning out folders or binders. It is suggested that you cover this area thoroughly with your students and make it clear which papers you want them to keep and which can be discarded.

No matter how good the system is, it cannot work on its own. Students must make the effort to put each paper in its proper place so that it can be easily found later. Any training you can offer your students in this area would be very beneficial.

## Suggested Strategies and Activities

- Require all students to use a uniform system of organizing papers. Thoroughly train them in the system. After a certain period of time, allow your students to evaluate the system and how it has worked for them. After evaluation, let them customize the system to meet their individual needs. Later, have them re-evaluate the system and any changes they have made.

- When training students in an organization system, offer visual demonstrations with a model folder or binder.

- At the beginning and end of class, remind students of where certain papers should be stored according to the system.

- Have frequent folder or binder checks, with an emphasis on neatness and organization. With a quick glance at an open folder or binder, you can offer a student feedback on how he or she is doing. Also, be sure to check for a proper label on the folder or binder.

- Have folder/binder clean-outs, perhaps every 6 or 12 weeks. Train your students in how to clean out their folders or binders. Guidelines for this are on page 18.

- Be sure to give your students adequate time at the end of class to put papers away properly.

- Educate your students' parents on the system being used by the class or on a suggested organizational system. Ask them to participate by emphasizing organization as they check homework.

# **Papers, Papers, Everywhere!** *(cont.)*

As a student, you have to keep up with dozens of papers each week. Tests, worksheets, letters to parents, and other important papers have to be organized so that you can find them when you need them. There are several ways to do this. In this chapter we will take a look at two different ways to organize your papers: using folders and using a binder.

## The Colored Folder System

1. You will need seven folders of different solid colors, each with pockets and brads (bendable tabs along the center that hold loose-leaf paper).

2. Label each folder for a different class. Also label each one with information about yourself, such as your name, school, grade level, and the name of the teacher of that class.

3. Put plenty of loose-leaf paper in the brads of each folder. If you need to keep other papers in the brads, then keep your loose-leaf paper in the back of the left pocket.

4. In the **right pocket** of each folder, keep all your assignments for that class that have not been graded. These are the assignments that you will need to turn in, including those you have not finished yet.

5. Keep all other papers in the **left pocket**, such as graded papers, handouts, grade sheets, and scratch paper.

6. Label one folder **"Home Folder."** Take this folder to every class and home every night. In this folder, keep things such as the following: class schedule, assignment sheet, notes from home, supply lists, daily schedule, permission slips, and other papers that have to go home to your parents. For more information on how to use a home folder, see page 17.

7. Label one folder **"Paper Supply."** Keep it full of loose-leaf paper and keep it in your locker. When you run low on paper in a subject folder, you can get more from your paper supply folder during a locker break.

<br>

| | | | |
|---|---|---|---|
| **Bob Wire**<br>Inda Middle School<br>**Mr. Lepton**<br><br>**Science** | **Bob Wire**<br>Inda Middle School<br>**Mr. Adder**<br><br>**Math** | **Bob Wire**<br>Inda Middle School<br>**Mrs. Past**<br><br>**Social Studies** | **Bob Wire**<br>Inda Middle School<br>**Mr. English**<br><br>**Language Arts** |

| | | |
|---|---|---|
| **Bob Wire**<br>Inda Middle School<br>**Mr. Adder**<br><br>**Reading** | **Bob Wire**<br>Inda Middle School<br>**6th grade**<br><br>**Paper Supply** | **Bob Wire**<br>Inda Middle School<br>**6th grade**<br><br>**Home Folder** |

# Papers, Papers, Everywhere! *(cont.)*

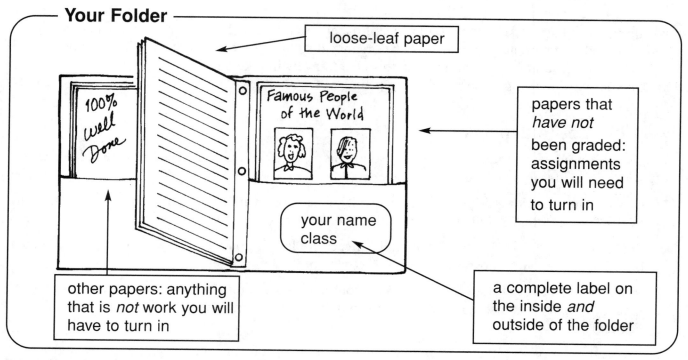

**Your Folder**

- loose-leaf paper
- 100% Well Done
- Famous People of the World
- your name class
- papers that *have not* been graded: assignments you will need to turn in
- other papers: anything that is *not* work you will have to turn in
- a complete label on the inside *and* outside of the folder

## Using the Colored Folder System

Now you have one folder for each class, and each one is a different color. Each folder has two pockets to sort papers, and brads with loose-leaf paper. Also, each folder is clearly labeled. To use the colored folder system, follow the steps below.

1. When you go to your locker in the morning before classes begin, get the books and folders you will need for your morning classes (the classes that you will attend before your next locker break). Also, be sure you have your home folder with you.

2. When you get into class, put the textbook and folder for that class on your desk. Put all other books and folders under your chair.

3. Any papers that you will need for the class should be in the folder on your desk. Papers that you get from the teacher and assignments you work on in class should also go into this folder.

4. When you open your folder, it should look much like the one above.

5. At the end of class, put away the papers from that class in the folder. Be sure to put each one in the correct pocket: papers that you are working on and papers that have not been graded on the right; all other papers should be on the left.

6. When you get a locker break, exchange the books and folders. Get only those you will need for the upcoming classes. Be sure to get the correct folders by checking the color and label.

7. When you visit your locker at the end of the day, get the books and folders you will need to do homework. Take those and your home folder home.

# **Papers, Papers, Everywhere!** *(cont.)*

## The Three-Ring Binder System

Binders can be very helpful because they make it possible to keep all your papers for all your classes in one place. To organize your papers within the binder, you can use dividers and create a different section for each class. In this case, all your papers will need to be punched with three holes, like loose-leaf paper, so they can be secured by the three rings. Another option is to use specially made folders, ones that come pre-punched with three holes along the side. These folders usually have a pocket on either side. Here are some guidelines for getting your binder set up:

1. First, you will need a sturdy ring binder, one that will last all year. Be sure to get one that is big enough to hold all your papers. Two- or three-inch (5 cm to 7.5 cm) size is recommended.

2. Label the outside of the binder with your name and other important information, such as your school name, grade level, and homeroom teacher's name.

3. Label each folder or divider within the binder with the name of the class.

4. Put the folders or dividers in the same order as your classes.

5. Have a separate folder or section within the binder for loose-leaf paper.

6. Have a supply of hole reinforcements on hand, those sticky circles that are used to repair torn holes in the paper.

7. Have a separate folder within the binder to use as a home folder. You can find out more about using a home folder on page 15.

## Using a Three-Ring Binder

Now you have one binder to hold all your papers. Within the binder is a separate section or folder for each class and a place to keep loose-leaf paper. Here are some guidelines for using your binder and keeping it organized:

1. When you go to your locker in the morning before classes begin, get your binder and the books you will need for your morning classes (the classes that you will attend before your next locker break).

2. When you get into class, put the textbook for that class and your binder on your desk. Put all other books and materials under your chair.

3. Any papers that you will need for the class should be in the proper section of your binder. Papers that you get from the teacher and assignments you work on in class should also go into that section in your binder. Be very careful not to put papers into the wrong section of your binder. For example, do not put your math assignment into the science section.

4. Take your binder to each class and take it home with you after school.

5. Take a few minutes each evening to look through your binder. Check to make sure all the papers are in the correct place, and that you have a good supply of loose-leaf paper.

# Papers, Papers, Everywhere! *(cont.)*

## Cleaning Out Your Folders or Your Binder

Cleaning out your folders or your binder on a regular basis can really help keep your papers organized. Do it at least once each grading period or as often as once a week. You will keep your folders or binders from getting overcrowded and heavy, and you might even find something that has been misplaced. Follow the guidelines below for cleaning out your folders or your binder.

1. Be sure the papers are organized before you begin. Check to see that each paper is labeled with your name and in its correct place.

2. Remove any papers that you do not need in the folder or binder. Throw them away or recycle them if you can.

3. Do not throw away anything you might still need. If you are not sure, check with your teacher. Check the date to see how old the paper is. This is one reason it is so important to label each paper properly.

4. Keep all graded papers in your folder or binder until the end of the grading period. If the teacher accidentally makes a mistake with your grade, it will be your responsibility to prove what the correct grade is. To do this, you will need the graded paper.

5. If your folders or binder gets too crowded, or if you do not want to throw away any old assignments, make a special folder or box for these papers and keep them at home. Keep only those things in your folders or binder that you really need at school.

## The Perfect Chocolate Doughnut Story

Once upon a time there was a student named Penny Perfect. Penny always did well in school. As a matter of fact, she always made 100% on everything she did. She saved every assignment and kept them in a gold-painted box in her room.

But one day the most dreadful thing happened to Penny. When report cards were handed out, her grade in science was 82%, a C. Penny was horrified and began to cry. Another student, Sally Sloppy, suggested that Penny check with the science teacher to see if a mistake had been made. Penny wiped her tears and blew her nose and went to see the science teacher, Mr. Lepton.

Mr. Lepton explained to Penny that her low grade was due to a miserable 71% on the chapter test. Penny assured Mr. Lepton that she had made a 100 on the test, that she always made 100% on everything. Mr. Lepton agreed to change the grade, but only if Penny could show him or her test with the 100%. Penny smiled in relief because she knew she had saved everything.

Penny found her science test in the golden box in her room and proudly showed it to Mr. Lepton the next day. Mr. Lepton apologized to Penny and changed the grade on her report card to an A.

Mr. Lepton felt terrible about his mistake and wanted to make it up to Penny, so he gave her a chocolate doughnut. Unfortunately, Penny dropped the doughnut onto Clyde Clean. But Clyde took it well, and simply said, "Don't worry Penny. Nobody's Perfect!"

# Papers, Papers, Everywhere! *(cont.)*

## Other Tips About Papers, Folders, and Binders

✔ Take the time to put your papers where they are supposed to go so that you will not have to waste time looking for them later. It takes much less time to put a certain paper in its proper place than it does to try to find a paper that has been put in the wrong place.

✔ Avoid keeping papers in your textbook. This makes finding the papers more difficult, and it increases the chance of losing them.

✔ On page 15, five academic folders are suggested. You will need more folders if you have additional classes, such as music or health. If your school uses a rotating exploratory schedule, you may want to label two additional folders "Exploratory #1" and "Exploratory #2."

✔ If you use folders, be sure each one is labeled thoroughly. If you lose a folder or get it mixed up with another student's folder, you will have a much better chance of getting it back quickly if it has a complete label.

✔ When a folder or binder gets worn down and begins to fall apart, replace it right away.

✔ You can keep things other than loose-leaf paper in the brads of your folder. However, papers kept in the brads for a long time have a tendency to fall out when the holes tear. Use hole reinforcers to repair the tears.

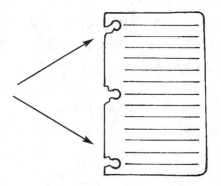

✔ If you use a binder to organize your papers, you must be especially careful not to lose it because it has all your papers in it. Be sure it is labeled completely.

✔ If you use a binder to organize your papers, you might use a separate folder as a home folder. Home folders are explained on page 15.

✔ However you decide to organize your papers, just be sure that the system works for you. If not, keep experimenting with different methods until you find one that fits your needs.

# Homework Helpers

Most students struggle with homework at some time or another. This is understandable, because dealing with homework can be a complicated process. First, the student must understand what the assignment is exactly, and write it down properly. Second, the proper materials must be taken home to complete the assignment. Third, the assignment must be completed correctly, which involves understanding the directions or questions or process, for example. And finally, the assignment must be brought back to school and to the proper class. Very often, this process must be done for several assignments at a time. And it becomes even more complicated when the student has been absent from school.

Because the homework process is so complex, it is essential that students write down their assignments at the time they are given by the teacher. This chapter shows students how to use a homework list to do this. An optional method, using an assignment sheet, is also presented. The assignment sheet relies on a system of parent and teacher support.

Even when thoroughly organized, homework can still be overwhelming when there is a large amount to be done. This chapter introduces students to the concept of prioritizing and shows them how to use it as a strategy for completing homework efficiently.

## Suggested Strategies and Activities

- Use the practice page in this chapter to have your students practice filling out an assignment sheet. For this activity, it will be necessary that you provide the students with fictitious information on classes and assignments.

- Require all students to use some approved method of listing their homework assignments, such as an assignment calendar, an assignment notebook, an assignment sheet, or a homework list.

- Require all students to use a homework list or an assignment sheet. Have them keep it in their home folders. The home folder is explained on page 15.

- As a morning activity, have your students label their homework list, or whatever they are using to list homework assignments.

- As an afternoon activity, prior to dismissal, have your students check their homework lists to see which books and folders they will need to take home to do homework.

- Give your students an opportunity to double check the accuracy of their assignment sheets by checking with a friend. Or, ask for a choral response to questions concerning the homework assignment(s) for each subject.

- Make assignment sheets and/or homework lists available in your classroom. Keep a stack of one or both in an accessible place. Remind students frequently that they are available.

- Suggest to your students that they choose a reliable friend to be a study buddy. They can call their study buddy to find out what the homework assignments are when they are absent, sick, or if they have questions about an assignment.

# Homework Helpers *(cont.)*

Many people have jobs that require them to do some of their work at home. Students have to do this all the time. Whether you are in college, high school, or middle school, you will probably have homework to do almost every evening. Completing assignments at home and getting them back to school and turned in to the teacher takes effort and organization. In this chapter, we will take a look at how prioritizing your assignments and using a homework list can help make this job easier.

## Homework Lists

Using a homework list can really help you to get organized. This simple method of listing your assignments takes the worries out of homework and puts you in control. It gives you a chance to get the assignments off your mind and onto the paper. Here is what you do:

1. Make copies of the Homework List form, one for each day of school. Keep plenty of clean copies in your home folder. The home folder is explained on page 15. The Homework List can be found in the appendix, which begins on page 131.

2. Each morning, before classes begin, label one homework list with your name and the date, and circle the day of the week. Then put it back in your home folder. This is the list you will be using for the day.

3. Take your home folder to every class and put your homework list on your desk at the beginning of each class.

4. When homework is given, write it down under *assignment*. Use the notes section to write anything special about the assignment. Take a look at the example on the next page.

5. Be sure you know exactly what to do on the homework assignment. You might need to ask questions to find out things such as when the assignment is due, how it will be graded, how many pages or words long it should be, and whether or not two students can work on it together.

6. At the end of class, be sure to put your homework list back into your home folder, not the subject folder for that class.

7. Take your home folder home with you. When you sit down to do homework after school, start by checking your list.

8. As you complete each assignment, cross it out or check it off. This will give you a chance to see your progress, and it will help you to feel good about getting things done.

# Homework Helpers *(cont.)*

## Homework List

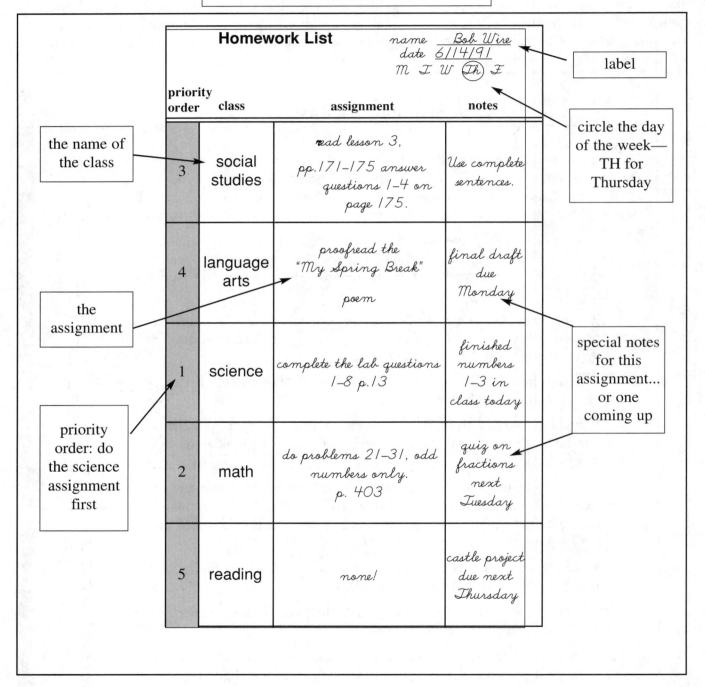

| | | | |
|---|---|---|---|
| | | **Homework List** | name __Bob Wire__  date __6/14/91__  M  T  W  (Th)  F |

**label**

**circle the day of the week— TH for Thursday**

| priority order | class | assignment | notes |
|---|---|---|---|
| 3 | social studies | read lesson 3, pp.171–175 answer questions 1–4 on page 175. | Use complete sentences. |
| 4 | language arts | proofread the "My Spring Break" poem | final draft due Monday |
| 1 | science | complete the lab questions 1–8 p.13 | finished numbers 1–3 in class today |
| 2 | math | do problems 21–31, odd numbers only. p. 403 | quiz on fractions next Tuesday |
| 5 | reading | none! | castle project due next Thursday |

**the name of the class**

**the assignment**

**priority order: do the science assignment first**

**special notes for this assignment... or one coming up**

# **Homework Helpers** *(cont.)*

## Prioritizing

*Prioritize* means to put in order of importance: the most important things first, the least important things last. When you sit down to do homework, start by sizing up your task. Use the *priority order* column on your homework list to put your assignments in order from first to last. If you have five assignments, for example, number them 1 through 5 in the order in which you will do them. As you will see in the guidelines below, the most important assignments do not always go first.

## How to Prioritize Your Assignments

1. Start with a short assignment or with one you like. This will make it easier to get started on your homework.

2. The longer assignments and subjects you like least should go in the middle. Try not to save these for last, or you might run out of time.

3. Assignments that are not due the next day should be saved for last. Extra-credit assignments should also be saved for last.

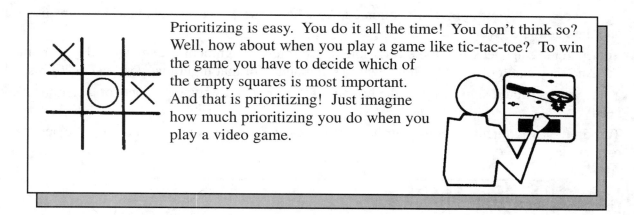

Prioritizing is easy. You do it all the time! You don't think so? Well, how about when you play a game like tic-tac-toe? To win the game you have to decide which of the empty squares is most important. And that is prioritizing! Just imagine how much prioritizing you do when you play a video game.

### Bob's Castle Project

Bob was really excited about the castle project in social studies. Even though the project was not due until next week, he spent four hours that evening working on it. Unfortunately, he did not do any of his other homework, not even the social studies work sheet that was due the next day. The next morning Bob did not have any time to work on his castle because he was too busy doing two days' worth of homework. Bob discovered how important it is to prioritize homework assignments.

# **Homework Helpers** *(cont.)*

## Assignment Sheets

The Assignment Sheet form can be used in place of the Homework List. The method is basically the same with both forms, but the assignment sheet relies on a system of parent and teacher support. If you usually have trouble keeping up with homework, then use the Assignment Sheet. Your parents and teachers will be more than happy to help.

## How to Use an Assignment Sheet

1.  At the end of each class, write in the name of any assignments you have worked on in class and the name of the homework assignment for that night in the *tonight's homework* box.

2.  Under *today's class*, write in the name of the class.

3.  Ask your teacher to check off any assignments that you have finished under *finished*.

4.  Next to *conduct*, your teacher may give you a grade.

5.  Next to *homework*, your teacher can write *yes* or *no* to indicate whether or not you completed and turned in any assignments that were due for class that day.

6.  Your teacher should then sign or initial next to *teacher signature*.

7.  When you finish your homework at home after school, show your parents your assignment sheet and the completed work.

8.  Your parents can check the homework note to see if any assignments due for that day were turned in. And they can look over the homework assignments for that night that you have just finished.

9.  Your parents should sign and date the bottom of the form and write comments or questions if they need to.

10. Turn in the assignment sheet to your homeroom teacher the next morning, and begin a new sheet for that day.

| **Assignment Sheet** | | name: *Clyde Clean* <br> date: *1/23/95* <br> M T W TH F | | |
|---|---|---|---|---|
| today's class | tonight's homework | | priority order | finished ✔ |
| class: *social studies* <br> conduct: *A* <br> homework: *Yes* <br> teacher signature: *JB* | worksheet *"Using Maps"* <br> finish questions 1–4, p. 183 | | 1 | ✔ <br> ✔ |
| class: *language arts* <br> conduct: *A* <br> homework: *Yes* <br> teacher signature: *WW* | study spelling words <br> for the test tomorrow | | 2 | ✔ |
| | | | | |

# Homework Helpers *(cont.)*

## Doing Excellent Work

Even when you are in a hurry, be sure to take the time needed to do quality work. If you carelessly rush through an assignment, you might end up having to do it again later, and that is a terrible waste of time. Keep these things in mind to ensure good work, and you can actually save time in the long run:

- Use good, readable handwriting.
- Use complete sentences whenever you can.
- Make your answers to questions thorough, using examples and details.
- Be sure your answers are accurate by double checking your work. This is especially important in math.

By doing these things you will save time re-doing assignments. You will also learn more from the work you are doing, which means you will not have to spend as much time later studying for tests.

---

### The Benefits of Keeping Up With Your Homework

There is one sure thing about homework: by doing all your homework on a regular basis, you will actually make your life as a student easier. Yes, that's right—*easier!* Here are some of the benefits:

✔ You will have **no hassle** from your teachers about late or missing assignments.

✔ You will have **better test grades** because you will have practiced the skills and studied the information through your assignments.

✔ You will have **better homework grades** because all of your assignments will be complete.

✔ You will be **more familiar** with what is going on in your classes, and that will make school **more interesting.**

✔ You will have **no make-up work** to do.

✔ You will have virtually **no worries** about schoolwork.

✔ You will **feel much better** about school, your teachers, and yourself.

---

# Homework Helpers *(cont.)*

## Practice: Homework Lists

Fill out the homework list below. Write in your first and last name, the date, and circle the letter for the day of the week. Fill in the names of your classes or subjects. Write in assignments and notes for each class according to the information your teacher gives you. Prioritize the assignments in the order that you feel would be best for you. Be prepared to discuss the reasons for your choices.

# Homework List

name _Caitlin K._

date _6/25/11_

M  T  W  TH  F

| priority order | class | assignment | notes |
|---|---|---|---|
| 1 | science | "Lights Out" Project due Monday | L3 Review due tomorrow |
| 2 | math | Chapter 17 Test Friday | Study |
| 3 | reading | Chap 5-8 20,000 Leagues Under the Sea | |
| 4 | language | None | Baggie Tale due next Friday |
| 5 | social Studies | Project Citizen Research | |

# Getting Set Up for Class

As your students move from classroom to classroom, they must set up their materials over and over again. Most students need training in how to get their materials set up properly at the beginning of class and how to make the most of those few minutes at the beginning of class. This brief chapter shows students how to set up a work area in a way that will maximize productivity. The idea, in a nutshell, is for students to get their areas set up quickly and efficiently and then to begin working on something independently. This will greatly benefit you as a teacher, in that your students will be practicing organizational skills and developing independence, both of which can help your class as a whole to become more productive.

## Suggested Strategies and Activities

- At the beginning of the year, train your students in the procedures you would like them to follow at the beginning of each class and how you would like them to set up their desks or work areas. The following is a sample set-up procedure:

  1. Check the chalkboard for instructions.

  2. Be seated and get your materials set up at your desk.

  3. Sharpen your pencil if you need to.

  4. Check on make-up work if you have been absent.

  5. Begin working independently.

- Post a chart which lists the set-up procedures for your classroom.

- To encourage your students to get set up quickly and independently, from time to time reward those students who get settled in diligently. Without drawing attention to yourself, issue a reward to each of those students who get set up quickly without a prompt. When the other students figure out what behavior is being rewarded, they will quickly begin to model the desired behavior. Rewards can be as simple as verbal praise, a token, or a sticker.

- Develop the same or similar methods of getting set up with other teachers who also teach your students. This will make it easier for your students to develop a routine.

- At the beginning of class, have an activity that your students can begin on their own. Write the instructions for the activity on the chalkboard so the students can read them as soon as they enter the classroom. You may even designate a special area on your chalkboard for this information. You may consider having the same type of activity each day, such as copying an interesting fact about science from the chalkboard, or making a short journal entry.

- As a demonstration for the class, let one or more of your students role-play the set-up procedures. Have them enter the class and go through all the steps for getting their materials set up and checking on make-up work.

# Getting Set Up for Class *(cont.)*

This chapter is about getting organized when you come into class. You can save yourself a lot of time and make your work more productive if you have a routine for getting your desk or table set up at the beginning of class. Here are some guidelines to follow.

1. Get seated right away and put these things on your desk:

- subject folder or binder
- text book
- homework from last night

- homework list or assignment sheet
- other materials you might need for this class, such as a calculator or colored pencils

2. Put all your other things under your desk so they are not in the way.

3. Sharpen your pencils if you need to.

4. If you have been absent, check on your make-up work.

5. Now that you are all set up, go ahead and get some work done. Here are some suggestions:

- If you had homework last night, check to make sure it is thorough and complete. If it is a writing assignment, proofread it. If it is a math assignment, double check your answers and look for careless mistakes.

- Many times your teacher will have an assignment for you to start on as soon as you get into class, one that becomes homework if you do not finish. Get as much done as you can now.

- You can also study vocabulary definitions, practice your spelling words, plan a project, organize your folder or binder, re-read a section in your textbook, or look through the next chapter in your textbook to see what is coming up.

- Your teacher's instructions about how to get set up at the beginning of class may be different than the suggestions made here, but the idea is the same: Get organized so that the things you need are on your desk and all of your other materials are out of your way.

## Your Desk

Your book is open to the chapter you are studying.

Your *home folder* is under your desk.

- subject folder
- homework list
- homework from yesterday

Your teacher gives you an assignment to start at the beginning of class.

SCIENCE
HOMEWORK
PLANETS
SATURN

# Managing Your Time

Many students maintain very busy schedules. After the school day ends, their activities begin, and they must also spend time doing homework and chores. Clearly, these busy kids can benefit from training in time management. Even students who are not so busy can learn to make more productive use of their time.

This chapter introduces students to these important time-management strategies: making a daily schedule, keeping a monthly calendar, prioritizing activities, being flexible with a schedule, avoiding an overloaded schedule, and making commitments. The importance of including a regular daily study session is also emphasized.

## Suggested Strategies and Activities

Have your students create a daily schedule of activities according to the guidelines presented. They can do this as a class or individually at home with their parents. Your students may also wish to make a schedule for weekend activities. A daily schedule form can be found in the appendix.

- Have each of your students make a list of all the things they can do in study sessions (besides homework) that will help them stay on top of their school work.

- Have your students brainstorm for things that can disrupt their daily schedules. Then have them list possible solutions for the schedule conflicts.

- Have each of your students list at least three activities that might take priority over a study session. Then have them list three activities that a study session would get priority over. Ask them to be prepared to defend their choices.

- Give your students a list of five activities to put in priority order with reasons for their choices. Examples: playing in a football game, cleaning one's room, studying for a test, attending a birthday party, watching a favorite show on TV, getting a haircut, cutting the grass, baby-sitting, etc.

- Have your students role-play situations where they have too many activities, and they let their parents, teachers, or coaches know about the problem and ask for advice.

- Have each of your students create a monthly calendar of important events in the current month. Guidelines for this are presented in this chapter. They can do this as a class or individually at home with parents. List any school-related activities that can be marked on their calendars. A monthly calendar form can be found in the appendix.

- Keep a calendar in your classroom with school-related events and important dates marked, such as tests, field trips, school pictures, holidays, dances, etc. You can also include a few interesting dates for things such as space shuttle launches, elections, and special events in history. Have your students check the classroom calendar each day and update their own calendars.

- When you announce the date of an important event such as a test, have your students mark it on their monthly calendars.

- Ask students to keep copies of their daily schedules and monthly calendars in their home folders.

# Managing Your Time *(cont.)*

Have you ever heard the saying, "There aren't enough hours in the day"? Sometimes it feels that way when you have a lot to do. Homework, concerts, projects, athletics, and chores around the house keep students very busy.

To make every minute count, you will need to organize your time. This is sometimes called *time management*. In this chapter, we will look at two ways to manage your time: setting up a daily schedule and keeping a monthly calendar. The daily schedule helps you set up a routine for an average school day. The monthly calendar helps you keep track of what is coming up in the weeks ahead. We will also take a look at how to be flexible with your schedule, how to prioritize your activities, how to avoid being overloaded with activities, and what it means to have a study session.

## Daily Schedule

Although each school day is a bit different, many parts of the day are the same, and it helps if they happen at the same time each day. You can do this by creating a schedule of your activities. Along with school and responsibilities in your home (such as chores), you will need to set aside time each day for homework, meals, fun, and sleep.

Use the Daily Schedule form in the appendix to create a daily schedule for your weekday activities. Keep a copy of your schedule in your home folder. (The home folder is explained on page 15.) Create a new schedule when your commitments change or when you start a new activity such as cheerleading or soccer. Here are two examples:

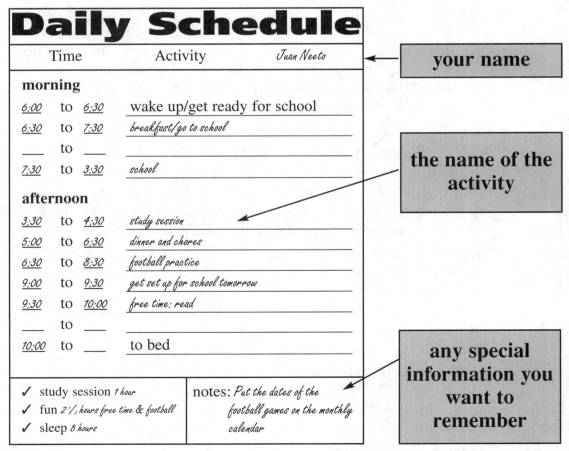

# Managing Your Time *(cont.)*

## Daily Schedule *(cont.)*

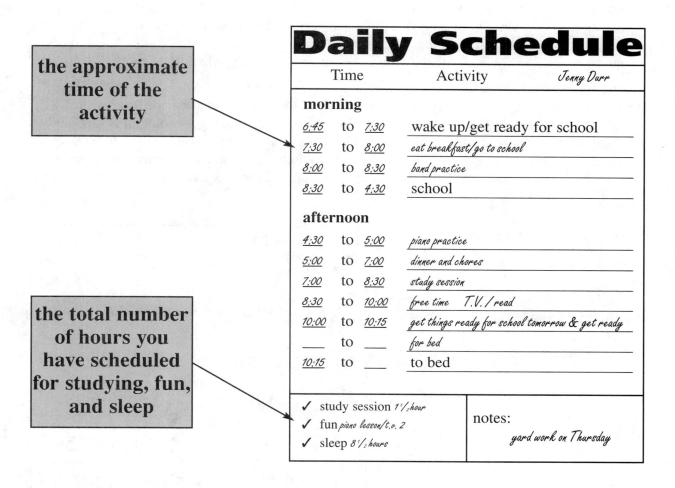

the approximate time of the activity

the total number of hours you have scheduled for studying, fun, and sleep

**Daily Schedule**

| Time | | | Activity | *Jenny Durr* |
|---|---|---|---|---|
| **morning** | | | | |
| 6:45 | to | 7:30 | wake up/get ready for school | |
| 7:30 | to | 8:00 | *eat breakfast/go to school* | |
| 8:00 | to | 8:30 | *band practice* | |
| 8:30 | to | 4:30 | school | |
| **afternoon** | | | | |
| 4:30 | to | 5:00 | *piano practice* | |
| 5:00 | to | 7:00 | *dinner and chores* | |
| 7:00 | to | 8:30 | *study session* | |
| 8:30 | to | 10:00 | *free time*  T.V. / read | |
| 10:00 | to | 10:15 | *get things ready for school tomorrow & get ready* | |
| ___ | to | ___ | *for bed* | |
| 10:15 | to | ___ | to bed | |

✓ study session *1½ hour*
✓ fun *piano lesson/t.v. 2*
✓ sleep *8½ hours*

notes:
*yard work on Thursday*

## Study Sessions

Set aside time each day after school to study and do homework. We will call this a study session. You can have your study session after school, in the evening, or in the morning. Try to have it at the same time each day. The best time for a study session is right after school while the lessons of the day are fresh on your mind. This also gives you plenty of time to complete your work. Starting your study session late at night or in the morning limits the amount of time you can spend on your assignments. Sometimes it is hard to tell just how long an assignment will take until you get into it.

Even on days you have not been assigned homework, it is still a good idea to have a study session which is at least an hour long. This will help you establish a routine for doing homework on a regular basis. During study sessions, there are many things you can do, other than homework assignments, which can help you stay on top of your school work. For example, you can practice your spelling words, study vocabulary words, work on an upcoming project, read ahead, or do extra credit work.

During your study session, take a short break and leave your work area for a few minutes about every half hour. The best time for these short breaks is when you are between assignments.

# Managing Your Time *(cont.)*

## Being Flexible With Your Daily Schedule

When you have a permanent change in your daily schedule, like starting gymnastics lessons, for example, you will need to rewrite your daily schedule and rearrange your activity times. However, when you have a small, one-day change, just "float" your activities around. That is, move the activities to another time temporarily. You can do this without rewriting your daily schedule.

For example: Juan has his study session scheduled for an hour after school, from 3:30 to 4:30. (See Juan's schedule on page 30.) On one particular day, however, Juan and his dad decide to go to the hardware store after school to buy lumber for a treehouse. By the time Juan gets home, it is 4:30 and he has missed his study session. Just for that day, Juan could move his study session time to 9:00 and study for an hour from 9:00 to 10:00. The next day Juan would have his study session at the regularly scheduled time after school. Being flexible with your daily schedule means making temporary changes as Juan did in this example.

## Prioritizing Your Activities

Just as you prioritize your assignments before you start homework, you will need to prioritize your activities during the day, especially when there is a temporary change in your schedule. This way you will be sure to get the things done that are most important, which is what prioritizing is all about.

Take a look at Jenny's daily schedule on page 31, for example. Jenny's study session is scheduled for an hour and a half, from 7:00 to 8:30. Jenny might have a piano recital in the evening at 7:00, which would take priority over her study session. Study sessions are important, but in this case performing at the piano recital would be even more important. She could then have her study session at 8:30 instead, when it would take priority over her free time.

## Avoiding Overload

When you feel overwhelmed with too much to do, be sure to speak up. Sometimes your teachers, parents, and coaches do not realize how many other responsibilities you have. Let them know how you feel: that you are managing your time the best you can, but there just is not enough time for everything. Show them your daily schedule and ask if they can help.

In some cases, you will simply have to limit the number of activities in your schedule. That alone can help you to be more successful as a student, and it will make your time much easier to manage. Prioritize your activities and decide which ones you can live without.

**Daily Schedule**     Name _____

Time     Activity

morning

_____ Wake up/get ready for school

Be Flexible!

_____

_____

School

afternoon

_____ to _____

_____ to _____

Prioritize!

_____ to _____

Avoid Overload!

_____

to bed

study session _____     notes

fun _____

sleep_____

# Managing Your Time *(cont.)*

## Monthly Calendars

Monthly calendars are a great way to organize your time, especially if you are busy with many activities. Keeping a calendar will help you to avoid scheduling conflicts with your activities or the activities of other people in your family. It can also help you prioritize the activities in your daily schedule and give you a chance to prepare for upcoming events.

## Keeping a Monthly Calendar

The first thing you will need is a calendar. If you buy a calendar, try to get one that begins with August and has the months in order of the school year. This will make it possible to mark the dates of events that happen after the new year (e.g. "school pictures," January 25).

You can make your own calendar by using the Monthly Calendar form in the appendix in the back of this book. Make twelve copies of the calendar form and write in the name of the month and the day numbers for each month of the year. Start with August and continue on through July of the next year. Use a yearly calendar to check the correct day numbers.

Write the dates of events on your calendar with information such as the name of the event, the time, and the place. Take a look at the example on the next page. The events can be school-related or extracurricular. Anything that is not a regular part of your daily schedule should be marked on your calendar. Things such as major tests and project due-dates should also be marked on your calendar.

At the beginning of the year, your teacher may give you a list of events for the school year. Dates such as holidays, vacations, open house, school pictures, and standardized testing can be marked on your calendar right away.

Be sure your parents are familiar with the events on your calendar, and their dates and times. Remind them often about events that require their help, such as chaperoning a field trip or driving you to school early for a club meeting. Also, let them know about any changes on your calendar as soon as possible.

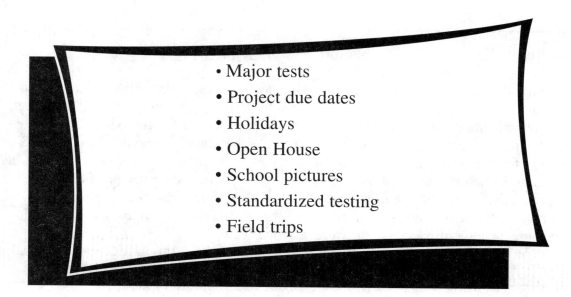

- Major tests
- Project due dates
- Holidays
- Open House
- School pictures
- Standardized testing
- Field trips

# Managing Your Time *(cont.)*

## Keeping a Monthly Calendar *(cont.)*

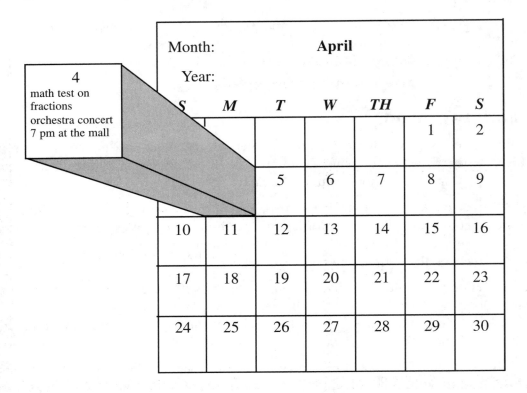

**Month:** **April**

**Year:**

| S | M | T | W | TH | F | S |
|---|---|---|---|----|---|---|
|   |   |   |   |    | 1 | 2 |
|   | 5 | 6 | 7 | 8 | 9 | |
| 10 | 11 | 12 | 13 | 14 | 15 | 16 |
| 17 | 18 | 19 | 20 | 21 | 22 | 23 |
| 24 | 25 | 26 | 27 | 28 | 29 | 30 |

The callout box reads:
> **4**
> math test on fractions
> orchestra concert 7 pm at the mall

## Making Commitments

Check your calendar before making a commitment to participate in an activity. Look to see if there is anything else marked on your calendar that would interfere with the activity. In the following example, Tasha checks her calendar before making a commitment to attend an extra softball practice.

---

### Committed to the Team

Tasha's softball team usually practiced every Monday, Wednesday, and Friday. In order to get ready for the play-offs, however, the coach wanted to have a few extra practices. The coach asked the team members if they could come to an extra practice next Tuesday. Tasha's monthly calendar was at home, but she was pretty sure that there was nothing else marked on her calendar for that day. Just to be sure, she told the coach that she would need to check her calendar at home before she could make a commitment to attend the extra practice. When Tasha got home after practice, she checked her calendar and saw that she was right; there were no other activities marked on her calendar for next Tuesday. After checking with her dad to be sure he could drive her to the extra practice, Tasha called her coach and let her know she could be there next Tuesday. Then Tasha marked the extra practice on her calendar.

---

# Managing Your Time *(cont.)*

## Keeping a Monthly Calendar (cont.)

### Examples of Activities

| School Related | Extracurricular |
|---|---|
| Field Trips | Cheerleading Try-Outs |
| Club Meetings | Football Games |
| Projects | Party at a Friend's |
| Tests | Camping Weekend |
| Concerts | Scouts |

## Other Tips About Time Management

✔ On a day that you do not have any assignments for homework, you can use your study session to organize your materials, clean out your folders, and check your supplies.

✔ Try office supply stores for a wide selection of calendars.

✔ Use a pencil when marking information on your calendar. This will make it easier to make changes later.

✔ Check your calendar in the morning each day before you leave for school. Frequently check the months coming up.

✔ If you have two events scheduled at the same time, be sure to let the people involved know about the conflict. For example, if the date of your hockey game gets changed to the night of your chorus concert, let your hockey coach and your chorus director know about the problem.

# Being the Messenger

Throughout the year students are asked to be the messenger between the school and their parents. The school sends numerous papers home every month, and many of these papers have to be returned to the school with a parent response, such as a signature. In this chapter these papers are referred to as *parent papers*. A system of managing parent papers is presented, which involves the use of a *home folder* and a school zone. A home folder is a special folder that a student takes to each class and home every night. A *school zone* is a designated area at home, such as a bulletin board or a basket where students put parent papers when they get home from school. Combining the two strategies, students can establish a habit of taking important papers to and from school.

## Suggested Strategies and Activities

- Require each of your students to have and use a home folder. Suggest that they use a special color which will not get confused with any of their other folders. Before you dismiss your students at the end of the day, check to be sure each student has his or her home folder. Each student can show you his or her folder when leaving the classroom.

- When you hand out a flyer, newsletter, permission slip, or similar type of material, have your students put these papers in their home folders.

- Have each of your students keep his or her daily schedule, monthly calendar, homework list or assignment sheet, supply update list, and similar papers in his or her home folder.

- Educate the parents of your students on the purpose and use of a home folder. Suggest that they ask about the home folder each evening to be sure it is being brought home.

- As a project, have each of your students set up a school zone at home. Make a special bulletin board which lists the characteristics of a well-made school zone. Make it optional for the students to bring in photos of their school zones. Add those photos to the bulletin board display.

- Request that the parent/teacher organization of your school provide each student with a folder at the beginning of the year to use as a home folder. Special bulk rates or school-related discounts might be available. Alternatively, ask the parent/teacher organization to sponsor a home folder pilot program for your class.

# Being the Messenger *(cont.)*

Throughout the year students are asked to be the messenger between the school and their parents. Dozens of papers are sent home every year, and some need to be returned with a parent signature. We will call these *parent papers*. Using your home folder and the method below, you can be sure to get every paper home (and back, if necessary) every time.

## Making a Home Folder

A home folder is a special folder that you take to each class and home every night. Label a folder on the front and back with your name, the name of your school, your grade, and the name of your homeroom teacher. Write **"HOME FOLDER"** in big letters on the front and the back. Inside this folder, keep papers such as these: parent papers, class schedule, daily schedule, monthly calendar, homework list, and supply list.

## Using a Home Folder and a School Zone

Choose a special place at home where you can always put parent papers, a place your parents will check everyday. It could be a basket or a bulletin board. Give this place a name. We will call it the *school zone*. Take a look at the example on the next page. The steps below show you how to use your home folder and your school zone together.

1. At school, put the parent papers that you receive in your home folder as soon as you get them.

2. As soon as you get home, put the papers in your school zone.

3. When your parents get home, they should check your school zone and sign the papers that have to go back to school.

4. Check the school zone sometime before you leave for school the next day, and put the signed parent papers in your home folder.

5. When you get to school, give the signed papers to your teacher.

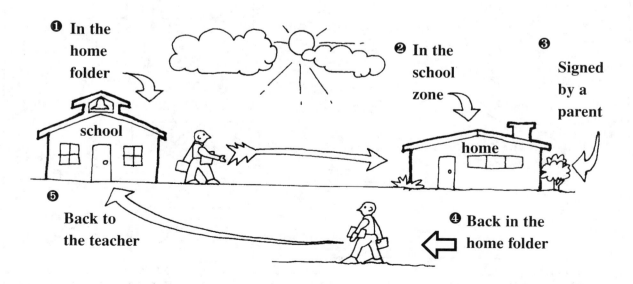

# Being the Messenger *(cont.)*

## Other Tips About Communication Between School and Home

✔ The school zone is also a great place for things such as lunch money, picture money, and notes to the teacher.

✔ To remind yourself about something important, you can leave yourself a note in the school zone. Since you check it everyday, you will be sure to get the message.

✔ If your parents leave before you do in the morning, be sure to check the school zone before they are gone, just to be sure they have signed any parent papers that have to be returned to school.

✔ Keep your school zone neat and clean. Remove any papers that are old and outdated.

## Example of a School Zone

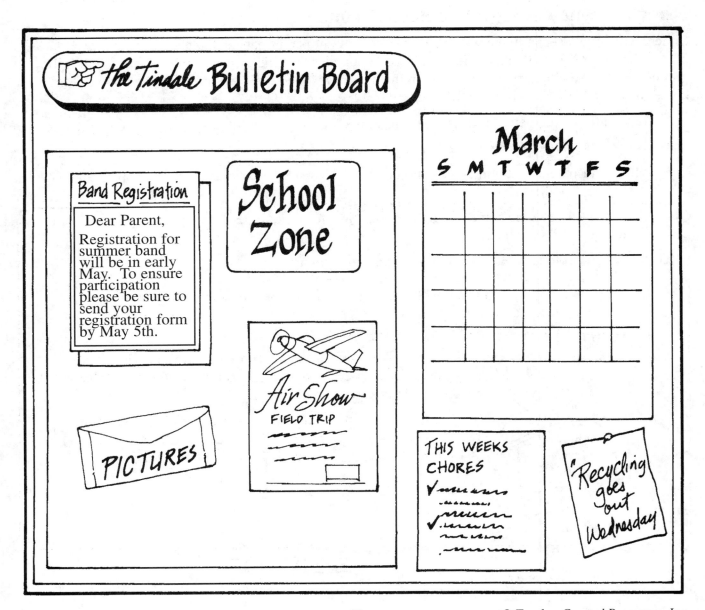

# A Place to Study

This chapter is designed to help students develop work areas that are conductive to learning. Many students fail to realize how much their efficiency suffers because of unfavorable studying conditions. Given the proper environment, these students could get more accomplished in less time. In this chapter your students will evaluate their current work areas with the help of a survey and class discussion. Then each student can begin building his or her own work area or improve an existing one. Encourage your students to include their parents in the planning and creating of their work areas.

This chapter makes two assumptions. First, the ideal work area is presented as one that is quiet and structured. Given the variety of learning styles, this might not be the best environment for everyone. Of course, many students will claim they do their best studying in front of the television, even when they know that is not so. It is important, then, that your students are honest with themselves in determining what studying conditions are best for them. They should ask themselves: "Could I save time on homework if the conditions under which I study were different?" Chances are this question will encourage them to be honest with themselves when it comes to their work area conditions.

The second assumption is that students have the resources available to develop a proper work area. It is understood that an individual student's family may be unable or unwilling to devote resources to the development of a work area. Realistically, for some students the kitchen table or the bedroom floor may be the only places available. However, there are many elements of a work area that these students may still be able to modify, such as lighting or noise level. And perhaps just knowing what qualities make a good work area can benefit these students later when their situations change and they have more control over their work area conditions.

## Suggested Strategies and Activities

- Have your students complete the survey on page 41. This will give them an opportunity to evaluate the effectiveness of their work areas at home. Lead the students in a discussion about what makes a work area effective. Your students may want to share ideas that have worked well for them.

- Have each of your students describe his or her ideal work area and compile a wish list of items that would make that work area complete. Each item on the wish list should be justified with an explanation as to why it is needed.

- Have each of your students devise a step-by-step plan for creating his or her ideal work area. Encourage your students to do this with their parents. Have your students explain in essay form how their ideal work areas could help them to be more productive students.

# A Place to Study *(cont.)*

A student's work is very much like that of a business professional. You have papers to keep up with, a schedule to keep, and projects to work on. Like any business person, you need an office or a work area where you can store your materials and do your studying. Having a good place to study can save you time on homework and help you make the most of your study sessions.

You may already have a work area set up. If not, we will put one up together. Let's start with a few questions to find out where you are doing your homework now. Complete the survey on the next page.

As you can tell from the survey questions, the best place for a work area is in a quiet, well-lit room, one without distractions, such as the television or people talking. You can set up your work area at a desk or table. If you do not have a desk, think about getting one. A desk makes it easy to keep your work area organized. With a desk, everything you need is right at your fingertips, and that will certainly save you time on homework.

Take a look at the work area example below. Desk drawers can be used to store materials, supplies, and graded papers you are saving. A dictionary, atlas, and other books can go on your bookshelf. Decorations can add a personal touch and help make your work area a comfortable place. Your work area does not have to look like the one in the example. Just be sure it is a welcoming place that helps you to be organized and productive.

## Student Work Area

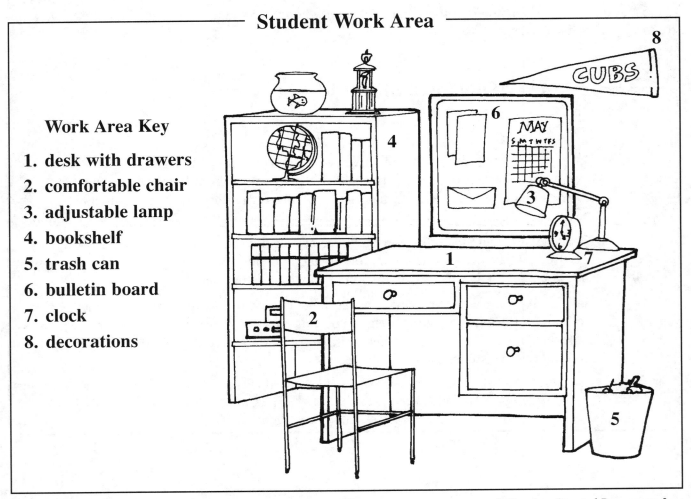

**Work Area Key**

1. **desk with drawers**
2. **comfortable chair**
3. **adjustable lamp**
4. **bookshelf**
5. **trash can**
6. **bulletin board**
7. **clock**
8. **decorations**

# A Place to Study *(cont.)*

**Practice:** Work Area Survey

Having a good place to study is very important because it can help you to be more productive during your study sessions. That means you will spend less time on homework, and the work you do will be of better quality. The questions in this survey are designed to help you evaluate your work area or the place where you have your study sessions. A study session is a time when you do homework and study.

1. Do you have your study sessions in the same place every time?

2. In what room of the house do you have your study sessions?

3. In what part of the room do you study? (on the floor, on a bed, at a table?)

4. Is your work area a comfortable place to work?

5. Is your work area set up like a work station or a miniature office with a place for your supplies and an area for you to do your work?

6. Is your work area a quiet place?

7. Can you concentrate while you are working there?

8. Is there plenty of light in your work area?

9. Do you think your work area is a good place to study? Why?

10. Do you like studying there? Why?

11. What are some other things that are important to think about when it comes to a work area?

12. What can you do to make your work area better?

13. What are some things your parents can do to help you make your work area better?

## Other Tips About Your Work Area

✔ Avoid having things at your work area that could distract you, such as a radio, a television, video games, or a telephone.

✔ Check the supplies at your work area each week and put anything you need on your Supply Update List form. This form is explained on page 7.

✔ Here are some accessories and supplies you might want to have at your work area: paper, pens, pencils, colored pencils, markers, crayons, ruler, pencil sharpener, extra book covers, extra folders, scissors, tape, glue, stapler, staple remover, calculator, dictionary, thesaurus.

# Part Two: What's My Grade?

If you have heard the question once, you have heard it a thousand times: "What's my grade in this class?" This can be a very irritating question for teachers to hear for at least two reasons. First, because of their heavy work load, teachers seldom have the time available to drop everything they are doing and calculate an individual's average. Second, the question itself implies that the student is unaware of his or her average, and teachers, naturally, would like their students to be more in-tune with their individual performance and progress. Frustrations aside, however, teachers can take some comfort in knowing that these inquiring students are at least concerned enough to ask.

Even those students who do well academically often experience frustration and anxiety about their grades because they do not understand how all the numbers add up. They witness the grades on numerous assignments, but in the end they see their final grades as a matter of luck.

In contrast, a thorough understanding of the grading system can be very empowering for students. It provides instant feedback. It encourages self-regulation. It helps students to understand how grades are *earned* rather than "given." And it gives new meaning to the phrase "reality check." Students who can calculate their own averages will be more sensitive to the devastating effects of a "zero." They will be more likely to understand how easy it is for an average to drop, as well as what it takes to bring an average up. Granted, it does take time and effort to educate students on the mechanics of a particular grading system. However, in the long run you and your students may find it well worth the trouble.

Educating students about the grading system in use is the focus of part two of this book. Two general systems are presented: a point system and a percentage system. A grade sheet is provided for each system, along with instructions on how to log in assessment grades on the grade sheets and how to calculate overall grade averages. You may find that neither system presented conforms to the one you use. If that is the case, please feel free to modify the ideas presented here in order to create a grade sheet and method that will work with your grading system. Also included in this part is information about letter grades and grading periods.

## Part Two

Chapter 9: **The Point Grading System shows** students how to keep track of their own grades under a point system.

Chapter 10: **The Percentage Grading System** shows students how to keep track of their grades when the grades are weighted.

Chapter 11: **Letter Grades** explains how percentage grades translate into letter grades.

Chapter 12: **Grading Periods** emphasizes the importance of knowing when each grading periods ends and shows students how to map out the grading periods for their school.

# What's My Grade? *(cont.)*

## Suggested Strategies and Activities for Part Two

- Provide each student with an explanation of your grading system and instructions for calculating averages. Demonstrate how your system works with examples and allow the students to practice. Several practice pages are provided throughout these chapters for the systems presented.

- To complete the exercises in this section, your students will need to be provided with certain hypothetical information, such as assignment titles, assignment grades, grade categories, and grade weightings.

- Provide each student with a grade sheet. Require your students to log in their assignment grades onto their grade sheets. You may want to require your students to share their grade sheets with their parents and obtain a parent signature. In this way the grade sheet can serve as a progress report.

- Post the percentages of your grade weightings.

- Post the grading scale for your school, indicating the percentage ranges for letter grades.

- For extra practice, distribute copies of a grade sheet that is partially filled up with grades, and have your students figure out the overall grade average.

- Have your students use the chart provided on page 53 to map out the grading periods. You may want your students to make two copies of the chart, one to keep at school and one to post at home.

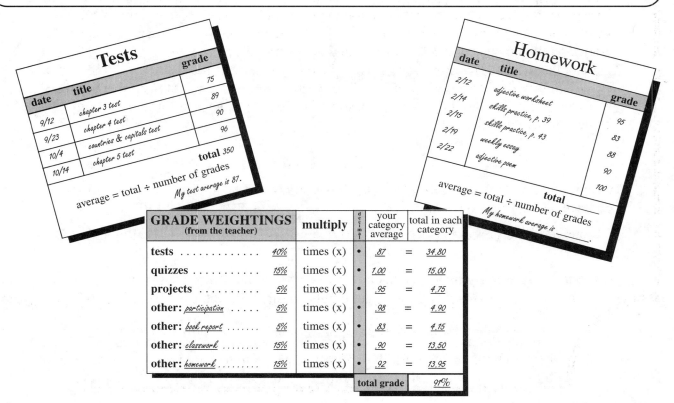

**Tests**

| date | title | grade |
|------|-------|-------|
| | | 75 |
| 9/12 | chapter 3 test | 89 |
| 9/23 | chapter 4 test | 90 |
| 10/4 | countries & capitals test | 96 |
| 10/14 | chapter 5 test | total 350 |

average = total ÷ number of grades
*My test average is 87.*

**Homework**

| date | title | grade |
|------|-------|-------|
| 2/12 | adjective worksheet | 95 |
| 2/14 | skills practice, p. 39 | 83 |
| 2/15 | skills practice, p. 43 | 88 |
| 2/19 | weekly essay | 90 |
| 2/22 | adjective poem | 100 |

average = total ÷ number of grades
*My homework average is _____.*

| GRADE WEIGHTINGS (from the teacher) | multiply | decimal | your category average | total in each category |
|---|---|---|---|---|
| tests . . . . . . . . . . . . . | 40% | times (x) | .87 | = 34.80 |
| quizzes . . . . . . . . . . . | 15% | times (x) | 1.00 | = 15.00 |
| projects . . . . . . . . . | 5% | times (x) | .95 | = 4.75 |
| other: *participation* . . . . . | 5% | times (x) | .98 | = 4.90 |
| other: *book report* . . . . . . . | 5% | times (x) | .83 | = 4.15 |
| other: *classwork* . . . . . . . . | 15% | times (x) | .90 | = 13.50 |
| other: *homework* . . . . . . . . | 15% | times (x) | .92 | = 13.95 |
| | | | total grade | 91% |

# The Point Grading System

As a student, you earn grades on individual assignments like homework, tests, and quizzes. These grades are put together at the end of the grading periods to make an overall grade in the class. This overall grade is called an average, and it usually goes on your report card or progress report.

Many students are surprised or even upset when they see their report card grades, as if they had no idea what their grades were going to be. But grades do not have to be a mystery. You can know exactly what your grade is in every class at any time. All it takes is a little know-how. That is, you just have to know how your teachers calculate their grades.

Your teachers will probably tell you how they calculate their grades. If not, be sure to ask. Chances are, each of your teachers uses either a percentage system or a point system. In this section, you will learn how each system works, and you will have a chance to practice. And believe it or not, calculating grades is actually very easy. All it takes is some basic math: addition, multiplication, and division. And it is even easier when you use a calculator.

The point system of grading is very simple. Each assignment is worth a certain number of points. This is called the total points possible. The score you make on the assignment is called your total points. For example, a vocabulary quiz with ten questions might be worth ten points. If you answer eight questions correctly, then you make eight points. For the vocabulary quiz, the total points possible are ten, and your total points are eight.

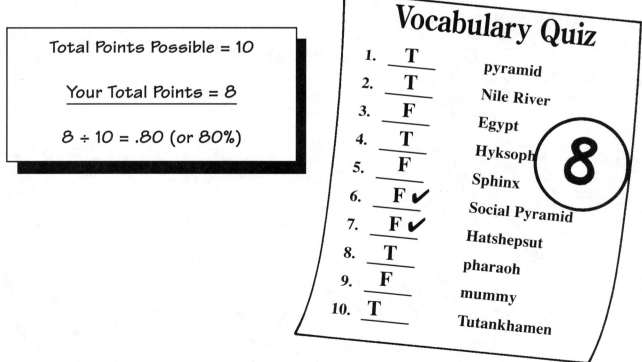

Total Points Possible = 10

Your Total Points = 8

8 ÷ 10 = .80 (or 80%)

## Vocabulary Quiz

1. __T__        pyramid
2. __T__        Nile River
3. __F__        Egypt
4. __T__        Hyksoph
5. __F__        Sphinx
6. __F__ ✔      Social Pyramid
7. __F__ ✔      Hatshepsut
8. __T__        pharaoh
9. __F__        mummy
10. __T__       Tutankhamen

To figure out the percentage grade of your assignment, divide your total points by the total points possible. In the case of the vocabulary quiz, your grade would be 80 percent.

Use the Grade Sheet for Points form to keep track of your points and grades throughout the grading period. Follow the directions on the back of the grade sheet form to figure out your overall grade in the class. You can do this at any time during the grading period.

# The Point Grading System *(cont.)*

## How to Use the Grade Sheet for Points Form

Take a look at the Grade Sheet for Points form in the appendix in the back of this book. When you receive a grade on an assignment, record it on the grade sheet. Take a look at the example below. Write in the date of the assignment, the title of the assignment, the number of points you received (your total points), and the total number of points that the assignment was worth (total points possible). You may also record the percent grade of each assignment in the right-hand column (% Grade). Also, if you need to record more than 25 assignments for the grading period, use an additional grade sheet.

| Date | Assignment Title | Total Points | Total Points Possible | % Grade |
|------|------------------|--------------|-----------------------|---------|
| 1/24 | book report | 15 | 15 | 100 |
| 1/27 | vocabulary quiz, chapter 8 | 8 | 10 | 80 |
| 1/30 | questions, page 154 | 4 | 5 | 80 |
| 2/6 | group project | 5 | 5 | 100 |
| 2/8 | lab, chemical reactions | 9 | 10 | 90 |
| 2/13 | chapter 7 test | 30 | 35 | 85 |
| | Totals ➞ | 71 | 80 | 88 |

To figure out your overall grade in the class, divide your *total points* for all the assignments by the *total points possible* for all the assignments. If there are more than two numbers after the decimal, just use the first two as your grade. Remove the decimal and add a percent (%). Take a look at the examples below.

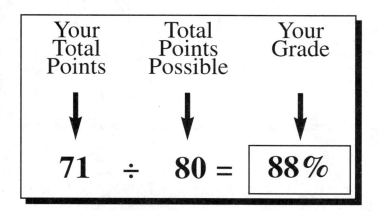

# The Point Grading System *(cont.)*

## Practice: Calculating Your Overall Grade with the Point System

Practice calculating the overall grade for a list of assignments provided by your teacher. Write in each *assignment title*, *the date*, *your total points*, and the *total points possible* for each assignment. To figure out the overall grade, divide your total points for all of the assignments by the total points possible for all of the assignments. The answer will have a decimal. Remove the decimal and add a percent.

| Date | Assignment Title | Total Points | Total Points Possible | % Grade |
|------|------------------|--------------|-----------------------|---------|
|      |                  |              |                       |         |
|      |                  |              |                       |         |
|      |                  |              |                       |         |
|      |                  |              |                       |         |
|      |                  |              |                       |         |
|      |                  |              |                       |         |
| **Totals →** |          |              |                       |         |

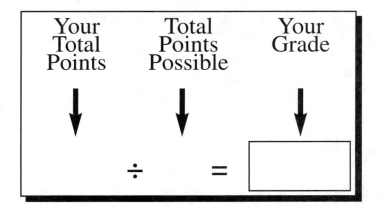

# The Percentage Grading System

Using the percentage system, the teacher turns each grade into a percent between 1 and 100. For example, if you take a math test with 20 problems, and solve 18 of them correctly, your grade would be 90% (18 / 20 = .90). The grades are then categorized by type, such as quiz, project, homework, etc. Each category is given a *grade weighting*, which is a percentage of your total grade. Most important categories (like tests) are given higher weightings than less important categories (like quizzes). If the grades were not weighted, then a short vocabulary quiz would count the same as a big chapter test. Take a look at the six categories and their grade weightings in the example below.

*Homework . . . 15%* means that your homework assignment grades make up 15% of your overall grade in the class.

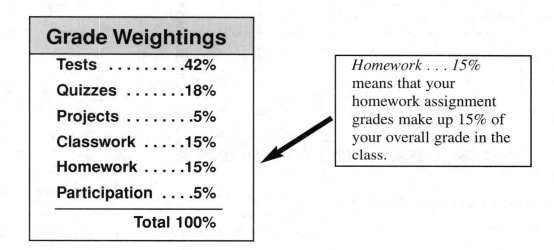

**Grade Weightings**

Tests . . . . . . . . .42%

Quizzes . . . . . . .18%

Projects . . . . . . .5%

Classwork . . . . .15%

Homework . . . . .15%

Participation . . . .5%

**Total 100%**

*Homework . . . 15%* means that your homework assignment grades make up 15% of your overall grade in the class.

Use the front of the Grade Sheet for Percentages form to keep track of your grades during the grading period. Follow the steps on the back of the grade sheet to figure out your overall grade in the class. You can do this at any time during the grading period, but you must have at least one grade in each category.

## How to Use the Front of the Grade Sheet for Percentages Form

Take a look at the Grade Sheet for Percentages form in the appendix. The front of the grade sheet has six boxes, each one for a different grade category. Three of the boxes are labeled *Tests*, *Quizzes*, and *Projects*. Label the other three boxes with the other grade categories used by your teacher. You do not have to use all six boxes. And if you need more room, or if your teacher uses more than six categories, then use an additional grade sheet.

When you receive a grade on an assignment, write it on the front of your grade sheet. Include the title of the assignment and the date it was completed. Be sure to put it in the correct box. For instance, a test grade would go in the *Tests* box, as in the example at the top of the next page.

To figure out your average for a category, add the grades together and divide the total by the number of grades. Take a look at the example at the top of the next page.

# The Percentage Grading System *(cont.)*

## How to Use the Front of the Grade Sheet for Percentages Form *(cont.)*

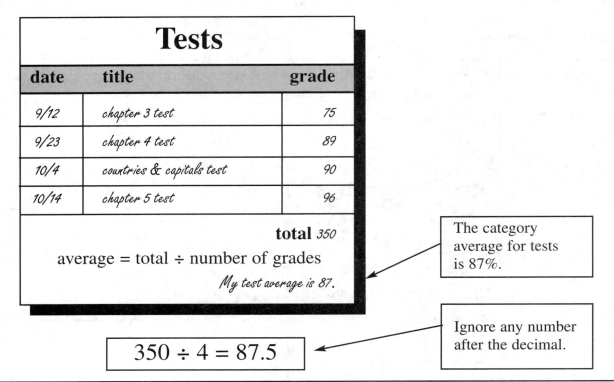

### Tests

| date | title | grade |
|------|-------|-------|
| 9/12 | chapter 3 test | 75 |
| 9/23 | chapter 4 test | 89 |
| 10/4 | countries & capitals test | 90 |
| 10/14 | chapter 5 test | 96 |

**total** 350

average = total ÷ number of grades

*My test average is 87.*

The category average for tests is 87%.

$$350 \div 4 = 87.5$$

Ignore any number after the decimal.

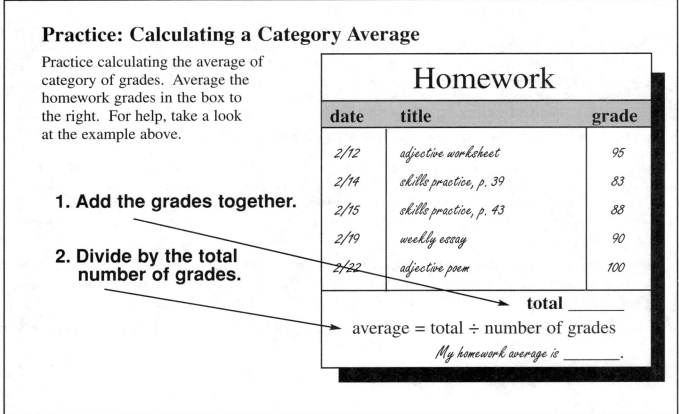

### Practice: Calculating a Category Average

Practice calculating the average of category of grades. Average the homework grades in the box to the right. For help, take a look at the example above.

**1. Add the grades together.**

**2. Divide by the total number of grades.**

### Homework

| date | title | grade |
|------|-------|-------|
| 2/12 | adjective worksheet | 95 |
| 2/14 | skills practice, p. 39 | 83 |
| 2/15 | skills practice, p. 43 | 88 |
| 2/19 | weekly essay | 90 |
| 2/22 | adjective poem | 100 |

**total** _____

average = total ÷ number of grades

*My homework average is _____.*

# The Percentage Grading System *(cont.)*

## How to Use the Back of the Grade Sheet for Percentages Form

Take a look at the back of the Grade Sheet for Percentages form in the appendix. You can use the chart on the back of this form to calculate your overall grade in the class. Follow the six steps listed on the form. Take a look at the example below.

Use the grade weighting as a number without a percent sign. Also, do not forget to add a decimal to the category average. If your category average is 100%, then just multiply the grade weighting by 1 (see *quizzes* category in the example below).

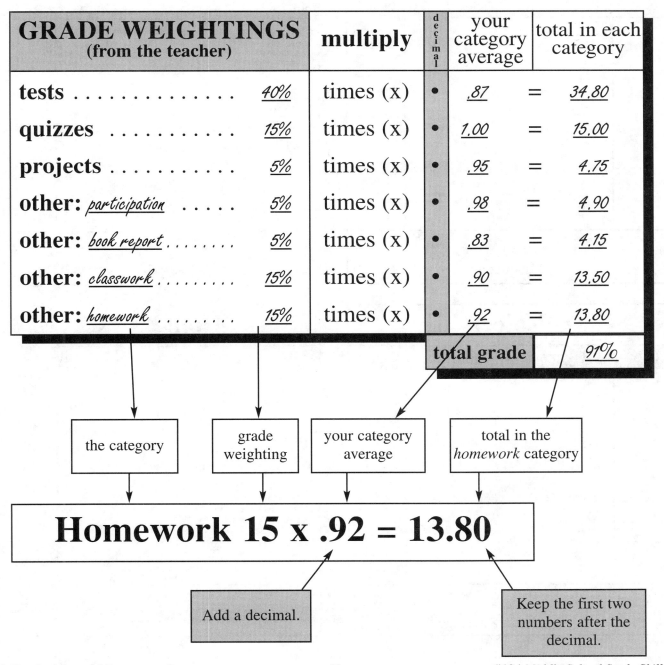

| GRADE WEIGHTINGS (from the teacher) | | multiply | decimal | your category average | total in each category |
|---|---|---|---|---|---|
| tests . . . . . . . . . . . . . | *40%* | times (x) | • | *.87* | = *34.80* |
| quizzes . . . . . . . . . . | *15%* | times (x) | • | *1.00* | = *15.00* |
| projects . . . . . . . . . . | *5%* | times (x) | • | *.95* | = *4.75* |
| other: *participation* . . . . . | *5%* | times (x) | • | *.98* | = *4.90* |
| other: *book report* . . . . . . . | *5%* | times (x) | • | *.83* | = *4.15* |
| other: *classwork* . . . . . . . | *15%* | times (x) | • | *.90* | = *13.50* |
| other: *homework* . . . . . . . . | *15%* | times (x) | • | *.92* | = *13.80* |
| | | | | **total grade** | *91%* |

the category     grade weighting     your category average     total in the *homework* category

# Homework 15 x .92 = 13.80

Add a decimal.

Keep the first two numbers after the decimal.

# The Percentage Grading System *(cont.)*

## Practice: Calculating Your Overall Grade with the Percentage System

**Part 1:** Practice calculating the overall grade for a list of assignments that your teacher provides. Write in the date, the grade, and the title for each assignment. Four categories are given in this exercise: *tests*, *quizzes*, *projects*, and *homework*. Calculate each category average. For each box, add the grades together and divide by the total number of grades. To figure out what the overall grade average is, complete part two of this activity on the next page.

## Tests

| date | title | grade |
|------|-------|-------|
|      |       |       |

total _____

My quiz average is _____.

## Quizzes

| date | title | grade |
|------|-------|-------|
|      |       |       |

total _____

My quiz average is _____.

## Projects

| date | title | grade |
|------|-------|-------|
|      |       |       |

total _____

My quiz average is _____.

## Homework

| date | title | grade |
|------|-------|-------|
|      |       |       |

total _____

My quiz average is _____.

# The Percentage Grading System *(cont.)*

**Practice: Calculating Your Overall Grade with the Percentage System** *(cont.)*

**Part 2:** Follow the steps below to calculate your overall grade in the class.

1. Write in the grade weightings that your teacher uses.

2. Write in your category averages from part one.

3. Multiply each grade weighting number times your category average. (Add a decimal in front of the category average number before you multiply. If your category average is 100, multiply the grade weighting number by 1.)

4. Put each answer in the last column, and add them all together to get your overall grade.

| GRADE WEIGHTINGS (from the teacher) | multiply | decimal | your category average | total in each category |
|---|---|---|---|---|
| tests . . . . . . . . . . . . . . . _40%_ | times (x) | • | _____ = | _____ |
| quizzes . . . . . . . . . . . _15%_ | times (x) | • | _____ = | _____ |
| projects . . . . . . . . . . _5%_ | times (x) | • | _____ = | _____ |
| homework . . . . . . . . _%_ | times (x) | • | _____ = | _____ |
| other: _____ . . . . _15%_ | times (x) | • | _____ = | _____ |
| other: _____ . . . . _15%_ | times (x) | • | _____ = | _____ |
| other: _____ . . . . _15%_ | times (x) | • | _____ = | _____ |
| other: _____ . . . . _15%_ | times (x) | • | _____ = | _____ |
| other: _____ . . . . _15%_ | times (x) | • | _____ = | _____ |
| | | | **total grade** | _____ |

# Letter Grades

Up to this point, we have dealt with grades as percentages. Chances are, however, you will want to know what letter grade (like A, B, or C) you have earned in a class or on an assignment. To find out how your percentage grade translate into a letter grade, follow the steps below.

1. Find out what the grading scale is for your school. It might be one of the two shown below.

2. On the back of your grade sheet form is a grading scale chart. Fill in the percentages that your school uses. Grade sheet forms can be found in the appendix in the back of this book.

3. If the grade you receive is a point grade, change it into a percentage grade. To do this, divide your *total points* by the *total points possible*. This procedure is explained on page 45.

4. Match your percentage grade up to one of the ranges on your grading scale. Your letter grade is shown on the left of the scale. Take a look at the examples below.

## Two Examples:

Your social studies project is a scale model of the Eiffel Tower made of toothpicks. Your teacher is impressed, and you receive a grade of 96%. (Using the point system, you might have earned 48 out of 50 points.) Using either the "modern" or "traditional" grading scale, your grade would be an A (see below).

On the chapter test, however, you score 81%. This would be a B on the "traditional" grading scale and a C on the "modern" grading scale.

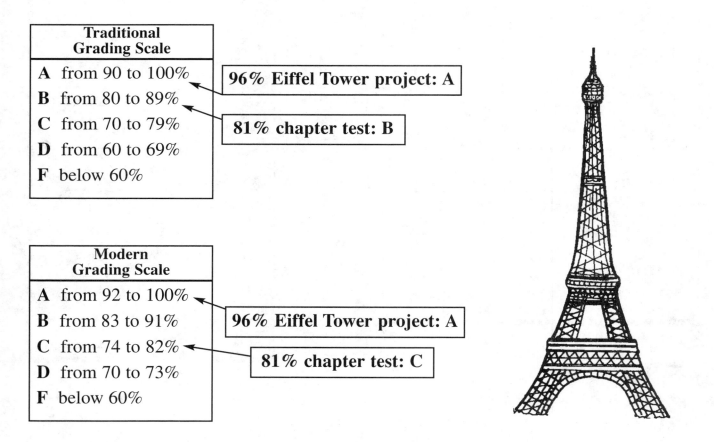

**Traditional Grading Scale**

**A** from 90 to 100%
**B** from 80 to 89%
**C** from 70 to 79%
**D** from 60 to 69%
**F** below 60%

**96% Eiffel Tower project: A**

**81% chapter test: B**

**Modern Grading Scale**

**A** from 92 to 100%
**B** from 83 to 91%
**C** from 74 to 82%
**D** from 70 to 73%
**F** below 60%

**96% Eiffel Tower project: A**

**81% chapter test: C**

# Grading Periods

Most schools today issue report cards at the end of every grading period. Some schools have grading periods that are six weeks long. Others have grading periods that are four, nine, or twelve weeks long. In some cases, only the quarter grades (grades after 12 weeks), or the semester grades (grades after 18 weeks), go on your permanent record.

It helps to be familiar with the length of the grading periods at your school. Mark the beginning and ending dates of each grading period on your monthly calendar. To avoid surprises, check your overall grade in each class halfway through the grading period or more often. If you find that your grade is low in one (or more) of your classes, give that class (or those classes) priority over the others until your overall average improves.

The chart on the next page is designed to help you "map out" the grading periods at your school. Fill in the beginning and ending dates of each grading period. The "notes" column can be used for things like the total number of weeks in the grading period or the title of the grading period (like Fall Quarter). Take a look at the example below.

| Grading Period | Start Date | End Date | Notes |
|---|---|---|---|
| 1st grading period | August 26 | October 4 | progress report |
| 2nd grading period | October 7 | November 15 | report card |
| 3rd grading period | November 18 | January 10 | progress report |
| 4th grading period | January 13 | February 21 | report card |

## Other Tips About Grades

✔ If your teacher uses a system of grading other than the point or percentage systems, create a grade sheet that will match his or her system. Ask your teacher for help.

✔ Extra credit is an excellent way to bring up your average. Before you ask your teacher for extra credit work, however, be sure you have completed all your regular assignments.

✔ If you have earned extra credit points, ask your teacher how you can figure them into your average and how to mark them on your grade sheet.

✔ Try to avoid making zeros on assignments (0% or 0 points). Even one zero can ruin your average. For example, three perfect grades and one zero average out to 75%, a C.

# Grading Periods *(cont.)*

## Practice: Grading Period Chart

Fill in the chart below with information about the grading periods used by your school. It is not necessary to use all the rows and columns. Keep one copy of this chart in your *home folder* and post another copy in or near your *school zone*. The home folder and school zone are explained on page 36.

| Grading Period | Start Date | End Date | Notes |
|---|---|---|---|
| 1st grading period | | | |
| 2nd grading period | | | |
| 3rd grading period | | | |
| 4th grading period | | | |
| 5th grading period | | | |
| 6th grading period | | | |
| 7th grading period | | | |
| 8th grading period | | | |
| 9th grading period | | | |

Notes:

# Part Three: Learning to Learn

For many students, the act of studying is as difficult as learning the information itself. This is because studying can be very complex. If often involves reviewing, organizing, and memorizing information. When studying, students must discern what information is most important. They must also evaluate their ability to recall the information they are studying.

In order to become proficient at studying, students must be taught study strategies, or ways to go about studying information. The ability to apply these strategies is often referred to as study skills. With practice, students can learn the strategies and develop the skills that will help make them confident, independent learners. Part three of this book introduces students to a wide variety of strategies that are designed to help them develop effective study skills.

## Part Three

Chapter 13: **Reading This and That** presents reading strategies that are designed to help students read more effectively and productively.

Chapter 14: **Take Note!** introduces a special method of taking lecture notes called questions-and-answers notes. Using abbreviations and symbols in note taking is also covered.

Chapter 15: **Memorizing and Remembering** offers a variety of strategies for memorizing and recalling information.

Chapter 16: **In a Word** is about studying vocabulary words and definitions.

Chapter 17: **Spell It!** presents a variety of creative ways to study spelling words.

Chapter 18: **Using Charts** demonstrates how charts can be used as tools for organizing and studying information.

Chapter 19: **Quick Writing** presents the writing process as a study skill and encourages reflection when completing a writing assignment.

Chapter 20: **This Is a Test!** includes strategies for preparing for and taking different types of tests.

Chapter 21: **Study Tips for Math** presents special study tips for mathematics.

Chapter 22: **Using Technology** offers some ideas for using technology as an aid for completing school-related tasks.

# Reading This and That

When it comes to studying, students probably spend more time reading than doing anything else. When students improve their reading skills they also improve their study skills. This chapter presents several reading strategies that are designed to help students read more effectively and productively. The strategies presented include reading differently for different subjects, previewing new reading material, taking reading notes, and keeping a personalized vocabulary list.

## Suggested Strategies and Activities

- Have your students categorize various literary examples as either textbook reading or leisure reading or both. Give them an opportunity to defend their choices.

- Ask each student to bring in an example of textbook reading or leisure reading.

- When you approach a new reading selection with your class, ask the students to try to identify which type of reading it is, textbook reading or leisure reading. Prior to reading, review with the students the strategies for previewing and reading literature of that type.

- Practice reviewing new reading material with your students as a class.

- When assigning independent reading material to your students, remind them to preview the reading first. You may want to preview the material as a class before assigning it as homework. This short exercise can help increase student interest and increase the likelihood that the task will be completed.

- Practice taking reading notes with your students, first with short excerpts, and then with longer assignments.

- Practice making a personal vocabulary list with your students. An exercise for this is included in this section.

- Keep a personal vocabulary list of your own posted in your classroom. This will inspire your students by showing them that you are also active in learning new words.

# **Reading This and That** *(cont.)*

When it comes to studying, you will probably spend more time reading than doing anything else. In this chapter, we will take a look at some reading strategies that can help you get the most out of what you read. We will look at how to read differently for different subjects, how to preview what you read, how to take notes while you read, and how to keep a personal vocabulary list.

## **Reading Differently for Different Subjects**

First, let's categorize reading into two different types—*textbook reading* and *leisure reading*. Textbook reading is reading about specific facts and details, such as dates, people, places, rules, and formulas. These facts and details are usually presented as part of a larger concept or idea, such as government. Some examples of textbook reading would be reading assignments from science, social studies, math, and grammar. The purpose of textbook reading is to learn specific things that increase your knowledge of a particular subject.

| Subject | Concept | Facts and Details |
|---|---|---|
| social studies | government | The Three Branches of U.S. Government:<br>    *executive*: the President<br>    *legislative*: Congress<br>    *judicial*: the Supreme Court |

The key to textbook reading is to read carefully and pay close attention to detail. It also helps to take notes as you read and read the assignment more than once. Look for things such as these when you are doing textbook reading:

- **vocabulary** words that appear in bold type and are found in the glossary, such as *democracy*
- **special terms** that are not vocabulary, that appear often in the reading, such as *cultural heritage*
- **places** that are important to the lesson, such as the *Serengeti Plain*
- **people** who are described in the lesson, such as *Golda Meir* or *Joe Montana*
- **dates** of events that appear in the lesson, such the *Reformation of 1517*
- **examples** that emphasize important points or demonstrate procedures to follow in an exercise
- **charts**, including graphs, maps, and diagrams, such as the *Periodic Table of the Elements*
- **directions** you are asked to follow in the reading, such as "Study the picture below."
- **theories** that are mentioned in the lesson, such as the *trickle down theory of economics*
- **laws** that are mentioned in the lesson, such as *Isaac Newton's law of gravity*
- **rules** that are important to procedures taught in the lesson, such as the *math order of operations*
- **formulas** mentioned or used in the lesson, such as *rate = distance x time*

# **Reading This and That** *(cont.)*

## **Reading Differently for Different Subjects** *(cont.)*

Leisure reading is very different from textbook reading. Leisure reading is reading for enrichment and enjoyment. Examples of leisure reading include stories, plays, novels, letters, poetry, essays, newspaper and magazine articles, and comics.

Leisure reading is generally *not* written to teach about a particular subject, although you may learn some facts and details as you read. For example, when you read a story about Robin Hood and Sherwood Forest, you might learn something specific about the geography of England or life in the Middle Ages, but the main purpose of the story is, instead, to tell about the life of the outlaw hero and his merry men.

When you are doing leisure reading, it is usually okay to read rapidly and focus on the overall story. Focus on things such as these when you are doing leisure reading:

- **setting**—the time, place, and environment in which the story takes place
- **characters**—the personalities in the story, especially the main characters
- **plot**—the series of events in the story and the order in which they occur
- **conflict**—the forces that oppose each other in the story, such as good versus evil
- **lessons**—the moral of the story: what the characters learn from their experiences

Sometimes it is difficult to tell if the reading you are doing is textbook reading or leisure reading. It could be that what you are reading is a little of both. Here are some examples of each:

| **Textbook Reading** | **Leisure Reading** |
|---|---|
| *Atoms and Molecules* | *The Three Little Pigs* |
| *World War II* | *A Day in the Life of the President* |
| *All About Nouns* | *Jane and Her Magic Tuba* |
| *How to Grow Vegetables* | *Buford Goes a Fishin'* |
| *Dividing Fractions* | *The Mystery of the Missing Zucchini* |
| *The History of Cubism in Art* | Poems by John Keats |
| *The Human Skeleton* | *Dear Abby* letters in the newspaper |

# **Reading This and That** *(cont.)*

## Practice: Textbook Reading or Leisure Reading?

Read the selection below and answer the questions that follow.

---

### The Nile

For centuries the Nile remained an obscure and unknown river. Even its earliest inhabitants did not know the source of its mighty waters. Not until rather recent (mid-1800's) British explorations did its myriad secrets surface. It is now known that the Nile is 4,200 miles or 6,720 kilometers long—that makes it the longest river in the world. The source of these waters lies at Jinja on the north shore of Lake Victoria. As it flows northward in a convoluted route, it drops thousands of feet along the way until it reaches its final destination, the Mediterranean Sea.

Even though the source of the river may have been unknown for centuries, the Egyptians made full advantage of the Nile. People were able to live securely in the knowledge that they were safe from intruders who did not dare cross the deserts that surrounded their fertile valleys.

Because of the annual flooding, the Egyptians were able to establish a fairly regular cycle of planting and harvesting. Excess crops were then exported, making Egypt a wealthy nation.

Animals thrived in the waters and surrounding land of the Nile. Goods were easily transported on barges and ferries. Probably the most valuable gift of the Nile was papyrus, a tall reed which grew along its banks. Papyrus was used to make paper, and Egypt was the sole supplier of this product until rag paper was invented in the twelfth century.

---

From TCM's "About the Nile," page 67, #292 Thematic Unit—*Ancient Egypt*.

## Questions

1. Do you think the selection above is an example of textbook reading or leisure reading? Give reasons for your answer.

   _____

   _____

   _____

   _____

   _____

2. What information and/or ideas from the reading do you think would be important to remember?

   _____

   _____

   _____

   _____

# **Reading This and That** *(cont.)*

## Practice: Textbook Reading or Leisure Reading?

Read the selection below and answer the questions that follow.

---

### The Santa Fe Trail

Wade looked over his shoulder at the shadows moving out from the hills, and he gripped the reins a bit tighter. It would soon be time to stop and make camp for the night. Once again there would be no fresh water, and the reserve barrel was only half full. Well, he shrugged, time enough to worry about that tomorrow.

From the back of the covered wagon came the sounds of his wife, Lucy Jane, moving utensils and belongings around in preparation for the coming evening. He'd warned her about the trip back at her parents' home in Virginia. "It ain't easy livin' out where we're headed—rough and hard on women and horses," he'd chuckled. "Reckon you can take it?"

"Don't you worry none about me, Wade Kincaid! I can take care of myself. You might just worry about improving your table manners a bit, though. Just because the country's hard on horses don't mean you have to chomp your food and slurp your water thataway."

The memory made him laugh. She was quick-tongued, but she was tough. She'd proved that when she set and bandaged her broken arm and hitched up the wagon herself after the trail accident three weeks ago. He'd been scouting ahead for game and water when it happened. When he got back, Lucy Jane was sitting in the wagon, pale but ready to go, a Winchester carbine cradled in her good arm. "I ain't holdin' nobody up on this trip," she said, chin a bit shaky. "Let's roll this wagon, Wade!" She had just celebrated her 17th birthday the week before on St. Patrick's Day in Independence on the east bank of the Missouri River.

"I hope you're ready to change that shirt tomorrow," she said. "That one's getting bit rank, don't you think?"

---

## Questions

1. Do you think the selection above is an example of textbook reading or leisure reading? Give reasons for your answer. _____

   _____

   _____

   _____

2. What information and/or ideas from the reading do you think would be important to remember?

   _____

   _____

   _____

   _____

# **Reading This and That** *(cont.)*

## Previewing What You Read

If you are reading something for the first time, it really helps to preview it first—that is, to look ahead through the pages and get an idea of what it is all about. Previewing gives your brain a chance to get ready for this "new stuff." Previewing really helps you get more out of what you read.

### How to Preview Textbook Reading

The way you preview your reading depends on whether the assignment is textbook reading or leisure reading. Textbook reading and leisure reading are explained on pages 57 and 58. First, we will take a look at how to preview textbook reading. To keep things simple, we will refer to the textbook reading assignment as a chapter. Follow the steps below when you preview textbook reading.

1. Read the title of the chapter.

2. Go to the end of the chapter and read the review questions.

3. Look over the chapter from the beginning and do these things:

    a.  Read the bold headings and the first sentence of each paragraph.

    b.  Read any special words in **bold type** or *italics*, and the sentences they are contained in.

    c.  Look at any pictures or charts and the captions (short sentences) that go with them.

4. Stop to think for a minute about the general ideas presented in the chapter, based on what you have looked at so far. If you are taking notes, try to write a few sentences in your own words on what you think this chapter is about. If you are not sure, then take a guess.

5. Read through the review questions one more time. If the questions are usually assigned as classwork or homework, go ahead and see if you can answer them now. Maybe you can only answer one, and even that might be a guess. But if you are right, you are more likely to remember that information later. Use pencil so you can make changes later if you need to.

Now you are ready to read the chapter. By previewing, you have "programmed" your brain to get ready for what you are about to read. The information will make more sense than if you had read without previewing. Also, you will remember more of what you learn from the reading, and that means less time re-reading and studying later.

If you are assigned the questions at the end of the chapter as homework or classwork, try answering them as you do the reading. Since you have already read the questions as part of your previewing, you are very likely to recognize the answers while you are reading. When you come across the answer to a question, stop and write down the answer.

# Reading This and That *(cont.)*

## How to Preview Leisure Reading

Remember, with leisure reading the focus is on the big picture and
overall ideas presented. Previewing your leisure reading can help give
you a "feel" for what that big picture is all about. Follow the steps below when you preview
a leisure reading assignment. To keep things simple, we will refer to the leisure reading
assignment as a story, even though many of these assignments are in another form, such as a
play, poem, or essay.

1. After reading the title, look to see who the author is and when the story was written
   (copyright date).

2. If you are previewing a novel, take a look at the picture on the front cover and read the
   synopsis which is printed on the back cover.

3. Check to see how long the story is and how it is organized. If the story is organized by
   chapters, read the chapter titles.

4. You may or may not want to look ahead and skim through a few parts of the book. If
   you are reading a mystery, for example, you do not want to accidentally find out who
   the culprit is before the story reveals it.

5. Take a minute and "soak in" what you have previewed. Make a prediction as to what
   you think the story will be about and whether or not you think you will like it.

Now you are ready to read. You can take notes if you want to, but try to keep them brief. Do
not let note taking interrupt your leisure reading too much. Remember, in leisure reading
your focus is on the big picture.

## Taking Reading Notes

Later on in this book you will be reading about how to take lecture notes or notes in class. You can also
take notes as you read. We will call these *reading notes*. It is a good idea to take reading notes when
you are doing textbook reading, because you are trying to learn specific information about a subject,
like plants and photosynthesis, for example.

The key to good note taking is not to write too much. You can always add more information later, so
try to keep it to a minimum. Focus on the main points that you are reading about. If you preview the
reading assignment first, it will be much easier to find the main points in the reading. There are many
ways to take reading notes. Let's take a look at one way to take reading notes called *outlining*.

# **Reading This and That** *(cont.)*

## Taking Reading Notes by Outlining

Outlining is easy and effective. It is kind of like making a "skeleton" of the chapter (or whatever you are reading), because you write down only the most important points. Follow the steps below for outlining and take a look at the example on the next page.

1. Write the title of the chapter at the top of the page in big letters. Add the chapter or lesson number and the page numbers next to or below the title.

2. If the chapter has an introduction, read it and write one or two sentences in your own words that sum it up.

3. If you are reading about a subject that you are familiar with, go ahead and write down a few things that you already know about the subject.

4. If the chapter is divided into sections, read one at a time. Before you read each one, write down the bold-faced title and place a Roman numeral next to it. If there are no bold-faced titles, then use the first sentence of each section or paragraph.

5. After reading each section, write down any important words under the Roman numeral and designate them A, B, C, etc. Add an explanation or definition of the words based on what you have read. Examples of important words would include people, places, and vocabulary words.

6. Write a sentence or two in your own words which sum up what you have read in that section. Label it with *SUM* for summary.

7. Write one question that a teacher might ask on a test about this section. Label it with *QUEST* for question.

Taking reading notes does take more effort than just reading, but it really pays off in the long run.

Here are some of the benefits of taking reading notes:

• Instead of re-reading the entire chapter, you can just read over your notes.

• Answering the review questions and any other homework related to this chapter will be easy because you have already outlined the important points.

• Studying for the test will also be easier because you can look over the questions you have made. You may see some of the questions you have made on the test.

• You will know the chapter inside and out.

• Sometimes teachers give open-note tests, which means you can look through your notes for the answers. When this happens, you will be in great shape with your outline.

# Reading This and That *(cont.)*

## Example of Taking Outline Notes

| *YourTextbook* | *Chapter 8* |
|---|---|

# Ancient Greece

**Introduction:** Today's civilization owes much to the ancient Greeks. With its rich art and literature and its democratic goverment, ancient Greece created the foundation upon which much of modern civilization is built.

## The Aegean World

The civilization of ancient Greece grew up in the "Aegean World." The "Aegean World" is the region surrounding the Aegean Sea and includes the shores of Europe and Asia (see adjacent map). This land is made up of many peninsulas and islands. High mountain ranges and narrow valleys characterize the landscape.

Built as a temple to the goddess Athena in 438 B.C., the Parthenon stands atop the Acropolis.

| *Your Notes* | |
|---|---|
| ◑ | *Bill Bob Sharp*<br>*11/15/94*<br>*Ancient Greece, Chapter 8, Pages 86-96*　　*Social Studies* |
| | |
| | *Intro—Much of today's civilization is built on the accomplishments of the*<br>*ancient Greeks.* |
| | *What I Know—The Olympics began in ancient Greece.* |
| | |
| | *1. The "Aegean World"* |
| | *A. Aegean World—The lands around the Aegean Sea.* |
| | *B. Peninsulas—A body of land surrounded on three sides of water.* |
| | *SUM—Ancient Greece was located in the "Aegean World," which is made up of*<br>*peninsulas, islands, mountains, and valleys.* |
| | *QUEST—What are four geographic features of Greece?* |

# **Reading This and That** *(cont.)*

## Practice: Taking Outline Reading Notes

The paragraphs below are from a collection of common beliefs and practices in Shakespeare's England. Outline each paragraph according to the guidelines on page 63. Use the form on the next page.

# *Elizabethan Times*

## Heralds and Heraldry

Although heralds were more prominent during the Middle Ages than in Shakespeare's time, they still held an important place in the lives of the nobility. These men were concerned with the dignity and honor of the king, noblemen, and gentlemen. They organized all important ceremonies, particularly royal weddings, coronations, funerals, and certain ceremonial rites. They were official messengers of the king during war and peace, and they read royal proclamations to the general public. Their most important function, however, was to preserve the records of noble families and to grant coats of arms to men considered worthy to be called gentlemen. They were a kind of "social register" and "Who's Who" of their time.

## Signs

In Shakespeare's England, houses were not numbered. Instead, each house displayed a sign which jutted out. Usually it was simple and may have been in the shape of a bell, dragon, or swan. Many homes in England are still named this way, and the public houses display signs which have been passed down for many years. Some signs contained recognizable symbols; for example, there were the red and white striped pole for a barber shop and the red lattice windows of a tavern.

## Bowls

*Bowls* does not refer to containers (called basins in England) in which to mix up a cake. It refers to a favorite game in which a small "bowl," or ball (called a jack) was used as a mark at the end of a green lawn. The players roll their bowls toward the jack, and the one coming closest to it wins. When a bowl touches the jack, it was said to "kiss" it. Rather than being a perfect sphere, the bowl bulges somewhat to one side and is thus said to be biased, curving in an indirect course when it rolls.

From TCM's "Elizabethan Times," #614 *Interdisciplinary Unit—Shakespeare*.

# Reading This and That *(cont.)*

## Practice: Taking Outline Reading Notes *(cont.)*

Title: _____Page(s) _____

What do you already know about Shakespearean England? _____

_____

## I.  Heralds and Heraldry

A.  nobility—the upper social or political class  _____

B.  heralds— _____

Summary: _____

_____

Question:_____

## II.  Signs

A.  symbols— _____

B.  _____

SUM: _____

_____

QUEST: _____

_____

## III.  Bowls

A. bowls— _____

B. biased— _____

SUM: _____

_____

QUEST: _____

_____

# Reading This and That *(cont.)*

## Personal Vocabulary Lists

Another way to get more out of your reading is to keep a vocabulary list. The more words you know, the better you will be at reading, writing, and speaking. It is very simple. Just follow these steps.

1. Make a copy of the Personal Vocabulary List form, which is located in the appendix in the back of this book. Or just label a piece of paper, title it *Personal Vocabulary List*, and draw a line down the center of the page.

2. When you are reading an assignment, or when you are just reading for fun and you come to a word that is new or unfamiliar, write it down on the left side of the paper. Next to it write the number of the page on which it is found.

3. Next to the word write a short definition of what you think it means. If you are not sure, use context clues. That is, try to find out what the word means, based on how it is used in the sentence it is in or by clues in other sentences around it.

4. After you have finished reading, look up the definition of each word and write it on the right side of the paper across from your own. Include the part of speech, such as noun, verb, adjective, etc. If your definition turns out to be wrong, cross it out. If it is correct or close, put a smiley face or a star next to it.

5. Now that you have checked the definition of each word, review how each one was used in the story. This might help you understand the meaning of the word more clearly.

6. If at this point you are having difficulty understanding the new word, ask your teacher or your parents for help.

7. Keep your list to review the words later. Use the words every now and then in your writing or conversation. This will help make them a part of your regular vocabulary.

8. Another option for this activity is to use index cards instead of a sheet of paper. You can even make a flash card for each of the words. Flash cards are explained on pages 78 and 79.

Keep in mind that many words have more than one meaning and will have more than one definition in the dictionary. The way the word is used in the story will tell you which of the definitions to write down. The word *loom*, for example, as a noun means "a machine used for weaving thread into cloth." As a verb, however, loom means " to appear as a large, threatening shape." Which definition do you think would be correct for loom in the following sentence?

   *Having no more money to buy thread, Franklin sold his loom to a tailor from London.*

It can be tricky to figure out which part of speech a word really is. The word *coax*, for example, is a verb which means "to persuade by pleading or flattery." In the sentence below, however, a suffix is added and it becomes an adjective used to describe a voice.

   *The sound of the mother's coaxing voice caused the baby to smile for the photograph.*

If you are unsure about the meaning or usage of a word, make a note of it on your vocabulary list and check with your teacher about it as soon as you can.

# Reading This and That *(cont.)*

## Vocabulary List Example

| | | |
|---|---|---|
| ○ | *Suzy Que 6/1/94 Reading* | |
| | *Vocabulary List: Jane and Her Magic Tuba* | |
| | *1. enchant—making magic* | *verb; to cast under a spell* |
| | *2. tempo—how fast the music goes* | *noun; the speed at which music is to be played* |
| | | |
| | | |

## Other Tips About Reading

✔ If you are in a hurry and do not have time for a full preview before you read, at least glance through the assignment and get a "sneak preview." A quick preview is better than no preview at all.

✔ Write your notes neatly enough so that you will not have any trouble reading them later.

✔ You may want to keep some or all of your reading notes. If you study the same subject or read the same book at a later time in school, you will be able to use your own notes as a helpful source of information.

✔ You may want to ask your teacher to check over your notes every now and then. Your teacher can let you know if you are getting all of the important points from the reading.

✔ Ask your teachers if you can turn in your notes or vocabulary lists for extra credit.

✔ Read! Read! Read! Read as often as you can and as much as you can. Read for fun and read for learning. Reading will make you smarter and it will help improve your study skills. And that will help make school easier and learning more enjoyable.

# Take Note!

Taking notes is a life skill. That is, it is part of everyday life. Something as simple as listening to someone over the telephone give directions to a location and writing those directions down is note taking. Taking a lunch order for a large group of people, jotting down a phone message, and copying information from the television screen for ordering the latest kitchen gizmo all involve taking notes.

Of course, taking notes in class is more involved; yet it involves the same skills. Note taking involves listening skills and critical thinking skills. One must listen attentively, discern what information is most important, organize the information, and evaluate whether or not adequate information has been given and whether or not the information is understood. Sometimes the person giving directions over the telephone babbles on about irrelevant information that does not need to be written down. And sometimes the directions given are incomplete or confusing and need further clarification. In this case, finding the desired location depends, at least in part, on good note taking.

Through practice, your students can develop effective note taking skills. In this chapter, students are introduced to a method of taking lecture notes called *Question and Answer*, or *Q & A*. Students often find it difficult to effectively study their notes. With the Q & A method of note taking, students can easily quiz themselves on the contents of their notes. Also in this chapter are guidelines for deciding what information should be included in lecture notes along with tips for using abbreviations and symbols.

# Take Note! *(cont.)*

## Suggested Strategies and Activities

- For practice, play a recording of a short, slow, simplified lecture for your students and have them take notes. Do not pause or stop the recording during the lecture. Ask your students to write a certain number of items or bits of important information from the lecture. Have each student share his or her items with a partner or a small group. Offer feedback to the students as to what information from the lecture was most important. Replay the lecture to give students a chance to evaluate the contents of their notes and the information discussed. Repeat this activity, increasing the length, speed, and/or complexity of the lecture.

- Have your students take notes of directions you give to a certain location. Then, either individually or in groups, have them create a map detailing the route. Have them share and compare their maps.

- Another method of note taking (outlining) is presented on pages 63–66, as a way to take reading notes. This method can be adapted for taking lecture notes.

- You may want to give special consideration to students who have deficiencies in the area of auditory learning. They can benefit from a written guide to the lecture, a copy of your notes with certain areas blanked out that they can fill in, or a copy of the lecture on tape.

- The Q&A method of note taking presented in this chapter can also be used to take reading notes.

- Have your students leave spaces between note items so that other information can be inserted later.

- Students often get frustrated when taking lecture notes. They feel they have to write down everything so as not to miss something important. Explain to your students that it is not always possible or expected that they write down every important point. They should simply try their best to get most of the important information.

- You may want to have your students add pictures to their notes. This can be another avenue for expressing the ideas presented in the lecture. More information on pictures is presented on page 80.

- Engage your students in designing methods for note taking, complete with titles and directions. Encourage them to design methods that make it possible to study the notes effectively and independently. They can then share and compare their methods.

- Have your students brainstorm and create lists of commonly used abbreviations and symbols. Compare their lists to the one presented in the section. A short practice page is provided for developing abbreviations and symbols.

- A practice page is provided for taking Q & A notes. It includes a chart and a cover sheet cut out.

# Take Note! *(cont.)*

Taking notes in class is a great idea. It is like listening with your pencil. Taking notes gets you actively and physically involved in what is going on in class. It will also save your time. Because when you write down the important things that the teacher says, you are actually studying them, too, and that means less time later studying for the test.

Earlier in this book, you read about how to take notes as you read. Now let's look at how to take notes in class. These are called *lecture notes*. When the teacher talks to the class about the subject you are studying, it is called a lecture. When you write down the important things your teacher mentions, you are taking lecture notes.

## Q & A Notes

One way to take lecture notes is called Question and Answer, or Q & A. Q & A note taking works especially well because it makes it easy to study your notes later. Listed below are the steps for taking Q & A notes. Follow the steps and take a look at the example below.

1. Label a piece of paper and title it "Lecture Notes." Under or next to the title, write the subject of the lecture, such as "Chapter 4, The States of Matter."

2. Using a ruler, draw a line down the center of the paper. Label the left side *Answers* and the right side *Questions*.

3. Write your notes in the form of statements. Put the statements in the answer column (left side), and number them 1, 2, 3, etc. Skip two or three spaces between statements.

4. Later after class, write a question for each statement in the question column. The answer to the question should be the statement to the left. Take a look at the example below.

| | | | |
|---|---|---|---|
| ○ | *Dan DaMann* <br> *3/21/96* <br> *Science* <br><br> *Lecture Notes: Chapter 4, The States of Matter* | | |
| | *Answers* | | *Questions* |
| | *1. The three states of matter are solid, liquid, and gas* | | *1. What are the three states of matter?* |
| | | | |
| | | | |
| | | | |

# Take Note! *(cont.)*

## How to Study Your Q & A Notes

1. Cover the answer column with a card or a folded piece of paper so that you cannot see the answers.

2. Ask yourself each question from the question column, one at a time.

3. Say your answer aloud. If you cannot think of the answer, then guess.

4. Slide the paper down to reveal the correct answer (one at a time).

5. If you said the correct answer, put a check by the question. If you did not get it right, read the question and then answer aloud two times.

6. Do steps 1 through 5 for the answers that are not checked.

7. When you finish, check to see which answers have checks. These are the things you have learned.

8. Repeat steps 1 through 5 for the answers that are not checked. Eventually, all of the questions should be checked. (See pages 77–89 for tips on how to memorize.)

9. An hour later or the next day, repeat steps 1 through 8 for all of the questions and answers. Use a different symbol, such as an X to mark the answers you get correct.

10. You can quiz yourself with your Q & A notes any time. And do not be surprised if some of your questions are the same ones the teacher puts on the test.

| | | | |
|---|---|---|---|
| ○ | *Lecture Notes: Chapter 4, The States of Matter* | | *Dan DaMann*<br>*8/21/96*<br>*Science* |
| | | *Answers* | *Questions* |
| | | *1. The three states of matter are solid, liquid, and gas.* | *1. What are the three states of matter?* |
| | | *2.*    **cover sheet** | *2. Which state of matter has a fixed shape?* |
| ○ | | *3.* | *3. Why is it that a liquid does not have a fixed shape?* |

# Take Note! *(cont.)*

## Practice: Q & A Notes

Use the chart below to write five important items or bits of important information from a lecture or a reading assignment. These should be written on the left side under Answers. Then, on the right side under Questions, write a question for each item in the answer column. Study the items according to the directions on page 71.

| Answers | Questions |
|---|---|
| 1. | 1. |
| 2. | 2. |
| 3. | 3. |
| 4. | 4. |
| 5. | 5. |

# Take Note! *(cont.)*

## What Should I Write?

Many students are not sure what to write when they take lecture notes. The teacher talks and talks, and they do not quite know what is important enough to put in their notes. Being able to sift through all of the things that the teacher says and pick out the important points is not always easy. Here are some guidelines that should help:

1.  Only write down the main points of the lecture. If you try to write everything that the teacher says, your notes will either be a mile long or a big mess.

2   Listen for clues from the teacher, such as when the teacher says:

    *   "This is important."

    *   "This will be on the test."

    *   "Write this down."

    *   "Be sure you know how to spell this correctly."

3.  Look for clues given by the teacher, such as when the teacher . . .

    *   writes information on the chalkboard or the overhead projector.

    *   underlines or circles a word or a phrase.

    *   shows excitement about a particular point.

4.  When all else fails, ask: "Is this something we should put in our notes?"

5.  Many times a teacher will review the main points of his or her lecture at the end of class. This is an excellent time to check to be sure that all of those points are written down in your notes.

6.  Be sure to write down those points the teacher mentions which cannot be found in the book.

---

**Example:** The science teacher, Mr. Lepton, wants his students to know the definition of chemical bond, even though it is not in the textbook. He writes the definition on the board and makes an announcement to the class. "Knowing the definition of *chemical bond*," explains Mr. Lepton, "will really help you understand chemistry. It's not in the book, so be sure to copy it into your notes."

---

7.  Be sure to ask the teacher whether or not you will be tested on the information from the lecture which is not in your textbook.

8.  You should be writing about eight to ten statements in your notes per class, more or less, depending upon the teacher and the amount of information being covered in the lesson.

# Take Note! *(cont.)*

## Abbreviations and Symbols

One of the best ways to shorten the time it takes to write notes is to use abbreviations and symbols. You can use standard abbreviations and symbols, and you can also make up some of your own.

The most important thing to remember about using abbreviations and symbols is to be consistent: be sure that each abbreviation and symbol stands for the same thing each time you use it. For example, if "gr" stands for green in your language arts notes, then it should also stand for green in your science notes.

Take a look at the charts below and on the next page for examples of standard and made-up abbreviations and symbols.

| | **Standard Abbreviations and Symbols** | | |
|---|---|---|---|
| + | plus | e.g. | for example |
| @ | at | U.S. | United States |
| $ | dollar/money | < | less than |
| ¶ | paragraph | > | greater than |
| w/ | with | ? | question |
| w/o | without | = | equal to |
| $H_2O$ | water | ≈ | similar |
| p. | page | ≠ | not the same, different |
| pp. | pages | N | north |
| ch. | chapter | S | south |
| # | number | E | east |
| & | and | W | west |
| y | yes | ↑ | up |
| n | no | ↓ | down |
| SS | social studies | % | percent |
| LA | language arts | lbs. | pounds |
| SCI | science | b. | born |
| i.e. | that is | ca. | about, around |

# Take Note! *(cont.)*

## Abbreviations and Symbols *(cont.)*

### Practice: Abbreviations and Symbols

| Symbol | Meaning | Abbr. | Meaning |
|--------|---------|-------|---------|
| ↑ | up | exer | exercise |
| ↓ | down | rpt | report |
| → | through | prj | project |
| ☆ | important | supp | supplies |
| ✔ | check | wk | week |
| HW | homework | sent | sentence |
| Q & A | question and answer | RW | rewrite |
| comp | computer | $\Delta$s | pyramids |
| HL | homework list | peo | people |
| qz | quiz | diff | different/difference |
| voc | vocabulary | QE | Queen Elizabeth |
| DS | daily schedule | ME/NA | the Middle East and North Africa |
| FP | football practice | | |

## Practice: Abbreviations and Symbols

What abbreviations and symbols do you use?  On the chart below, create five abbreviations and five symbols that you think might be helpful to use in your note taking.  Include the meaning of each.

| Abbreviations | and | Symbols |
|---------------|-----|---------|
| | | |
| | | |
| | | |
| | | |
| | | |

# Memorizing and Remembering

A significant amount of your students' studying time is probably spent memorizing information, especially when they are preparing for a test. When studying to memorize information, students can benefit from a variety of strategies. This chapter presents memorization and retrieval strategies that are designed to help students learn information more efficiently. The strategies presented include flash cards, memory words, crazy phrases, pictures, and recordings, as well as general tips on memorizing and quizzing over material. Given the opportunity to learn and practice these techniques, your students will discover that there are effective, structured ways to go about memorizing information.

## Suggested Strategies and Activities

- Train your students in a variety of memorization techniques. Introduce one strategy at a time and give them a chance to practice. Encourage your students to evaluate the strategy based on its effectiveness and ease.

- When reviewing for a recall test (essay, short answer, fill-in, spelling), incorporate one or more of the memorization strategies into your lesson.

- Review the general tips on memorizing on page 78. Ask your students to contribute other helpful hints that have worked well for them.

- Practice pages are included for memory words, crazy phrases, and pictures.

- As an activity for using pictures, have each of your students illustrate an event or series of events from the lesson in comic strip format. You may want to attach certain criteria to the project, such as the use of certain vocabulary terms in the text.

- Have each of your students draw a detailed picture, perhaps a collage, which sums up the important points of a lesson, chapter, unit, or story. The picture should be accompanied by a written explanation or guide.

- Demonstrate how to make a recording for use with studying according to the guidelines on page 88. Include a demonstration of how to label the cassette tape and how to label the recording. Also demonstrate proper waiting time between items, such as spelling words.

- Allow your students to practice making recordings for studying. If cassette players are in short supply, allow students to work in pairs.

- When giving a test, allow your students to "unload" information on the back of their test or on a separate piece of paper before they begin. Unloading is explained on page 89.

- Working in pairs, have your students practice quizzing and being quizzed according to the guidelines on page 89. Special incentives can be offered to encourage students to work cooperatively. For example, students could earn bonus points if their partners do well on the quiz or show substantial improvement from the last quiz.

# Memorizing and Remembering *(cont.)*

Memorizing is a really big part of studying. Memorizing things such as names, dates, formulas, and definitions can take a great deal of time. By learning how to memorize better and faster, you will cut down on the time you have to spend studying. In this chapter, we will look at several methods of memorizing. But first, here are some general tips on memorizing.

1. Recite the information aloud. For example, if you are memorizing the order of operations for math, say each step aloud so you can hear yourself say it: "parenthesis, exponents, multiply, divide, add, subtract . . . "

2. Visualize the information. That is, create a picture of it in your mind. If you are memorizing the capital of Georgia, for example, picture the word *Atlanta* in your mind. Writing the information will also help you visualize it.

3. Memorize in short chunks. For example, if you have to learn ten vocabulary definitions, work on three at a time. After you have the first three memorized, or nearly memorized, go on to the next three.

4. Move as you memorize. Some people find it easier to memorize if they are moving, such as when they are pacing or rocking. Try this and see if it works well for you.

5. Memorizing is easier when you are able to concentrate. Study in a quiet, well lit place, one that offers the least distraction.

6. Keep checking to see if you have learned the information. Check and double check to be sure you have memorized the information. Having it "on the tip of your tongue" does not mean you have memorized it. Use this rule when memorizing: *If you can't say it, you don't know it.*

## Flash Cards

Using flash cards is one of the best methods for memorizing. It gives you a chance to focus on the things you have not memorized yet, without wasting time studying the things you already know. Follow the steps below for making and using flash cards.

1. Use index cards or construction paper cut into rectangles. The card should be thick enough so that you cannot see any writing on the other side.

2. In large letters, write a question on one side of the card and the answer on the other side. The question could be just a vocabulary word. The answer on the other side would be the definition of the word. You can label the question side with a Q, and the answer side with an A. If you are using cards that are lined on one side, use the lined side for your questions. Repeat this step for several questions.

3. Stack the cards with the question side face-up. One card at a time, look at the question and see if you can say the answer (without looking at the answer side).

4. Flip the card over and see if you were correct. If you get it right, put the card in the "YES" pile. If you get it wrong, read the question and answer several times aloud. Then try to say the answer without looking. Put the card in the "NO" pile.

# Memorizing and Remembering *(cont.)*

## Flash Cards (cont.)

5. After you have gone through all of the cards once, pick up the "NO" pile and try those again. Follow steps 3 and 4.

6. When you finish, go through the entire stack again. Follow steps 3 through 5.

7. Put the cards away for a while (10 minutes, an hour, a day). Go through all of them again the same way you did the first time.

8. For extra practice, try doing your cards backwards, like Jeopardy. Read the answer side and see if you can say the question.

9. Keep your flash cards wrapped up with a rubber band or bound with a large paper clip.

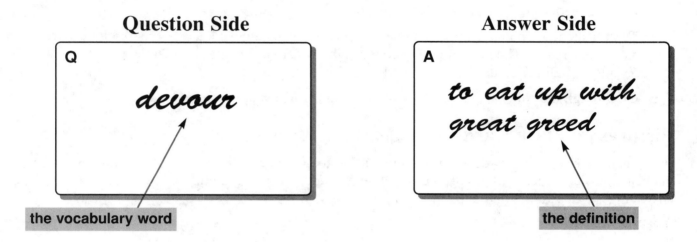

**Question Side**                  **Answer Side**

Q — *devour* — the vocabulary word

A — *to eat up with great greed* — the definition

The first time you go through the flash cards, you might miss every one. That is all right because as you go through the stack again and again, you will get more and more of them right. The "YES" pile will get bigger, and the "NO" pile will get smaller.

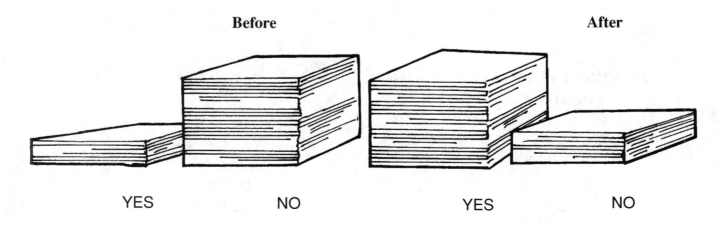

**Before**                                             **After**

YES            NO            YES            NO

# Memorizing and Remembering *(cont.)*

## The Ring Method

Another way to store and use flash cards is called the ring method.  This method makes the cards easy to carry and use, especially when you do not have a place to make a "Yes" pile and a "No" pile.  Follow the steps below.

1. Get a large ring that can be opened.

2. Punch a hole in the upper left corner of each flash card.

3. Slip the flash cards onto the ring, each facing the same direction.

4. Flip through the cards, studying them one at a time, according to the directions on pages 77 and 78, but without making piles.  When you go through the cards again, skip the ones you have mastered—that is, the ones you have memorized.

5. To indicate that you have mastered one of the cards, you can make a small mark on the card, such as a check mark.  The next time you go through the cards, skip the ones that are marked.  Eventually, all the cards should be marked.

6. Go through the cards again later (ten minutes, an hour) using a different mark.

## Pictures on Flash Cards

If you get stuck on a few cards and just cannot seem to get them right, try drawing a simple picture on the question side which will give you clues about the answer.  Later, after you have the answer right, try answering the question with the picture covered up.

**Draw a simple picture.**

**Imagine the picture you drew.**

# Memorizing and Remembering *(cont.)*

## Memory Words

Did you know that *radar* stands for *ra*dio *d*etecting *a*nd *r*anging, or that *laser* stands for *l*ight *a*mplification by *s*timulated *e*mission of *r*adiation? The words *radar* and *laser* are *acronyms*. An *acronym* is a word formed from the first letters or groups of letters of other words. In this section, you will learn how to use acronyms, like NASA (National Aeronautics and Space Administration), and abbreviations, like PBS (Public Broadcasting System), to help you study. We will call these *memory words*.

You can use memory words when you study. When you have several words to remember, make a memory word out of the first letter of each word. When you think of the memory word, it will help you remember the group of words. Take a look at the examples below.

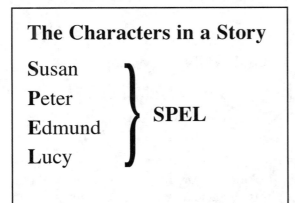

If the order of the words does not matter, then arrange the letters to make a word or something that sounds like a word. In the example above, The Characters in a Story, the letters are arranged to make SPEL. Say it like "spell" but remember that it only has one L.

If the order of the words in the group is important, then be sure to keep the initials in the same order. In the example below, The Stages of Metamorphosis, the letters are kept in order to represent the stages of metamorphosis from beginning to end. The memory word "ELPA" can help you to remember the stages of metamorphosis in the correct order. You will find that many of the memory words you make will be nonsense words, like ELPA.

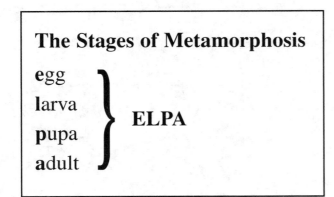

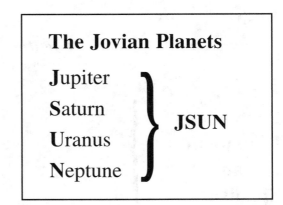

# Memorizing and Remembering *(cont.)*

## Memory Words *(cont.)*

Very often, the memory word does not have enough vowels to make it sound like a word or even a nonsense word, such as in the last example, *The Jovian Planets* (JSUN). Try adding some vowel sounds (just sounds, not letters) to make the memory words sound like a word. For the Jovian planets, you could say the memory words like "Jason," and think of the letters JSUN. Sometimes, the memory word does not have any vowels at all. Again, adding vowel sounds (just sounds, not letters) can make it *sound* like a word. Adding vowel sounds to the memory word below can make it sound like two words.

### *The Five Themes of Geography*

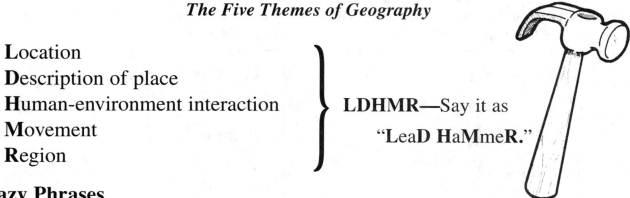

Location
Description of place
Human-environment interaction
Movement
Region

} LDHMR—Say it as "LeaD HaMmeR."

## Crazy Phrases

Another method of memorizing is called *crazy phrase*. It works almost like a memory word, but instead of making a word with the initials, you make a phrase or a sentence. The crazier it sounds, the more likely you are to remember it. Take a look at the examples below.

### *U.S. Presidents from 1970 to 1990*

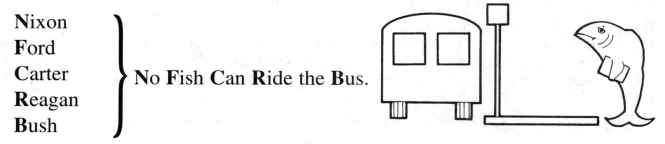

**N**ixon
**F**ord
**C**arter
**R**eagan
**B**ush

} **No Fish Can Ride the Bus.**

### *The Romance Languages*

**F**rench
**P**ortuguese
**R**omanian
**I**talian
**S**panish

} Fat Pigs Rest In Sludge.

# Memorizing and Remembering *(cont.)*

## Practice: Memory Words

Create a memory word for each of the following groups of words. Include a description of how the memory word should be pronounced.

| Group of Words | Memory Word | Say It Like |
|---|---|---|
| **Five Well-known Crustaceans**<br>lobsters<br>crabs<br>shrimp<br>crayfish<br>barnacles | **BLCCS** | **"blocks"** |
| **U.S. States Bordering Mexico**<br>Texas<br>New Mexico<br>Arizona<br>California | | |
| **Categories of Enzymes**<br>hydrolases<br>lyases<br>ligases<br>transferases<br>isomerases<br>oxidoreductases | | |
| **Baseball Greats**<br>Aaron<br>Morgan<br>Paige<br>Young<br>Ryan | AMPRY | |
| **Earth's Atmosphere**<br>nitrogen<br>oxygen<br>argon<br>water vapor | WAON | |
| **Greek Gods and Goddesses**<br>Zeus<br>Poseidon<br>Athena<br>Hera<br>Demeter | Zaphd<br>Phadz | |

# Memorizing and Remembering *(cont.)*

## Practice: Crazy Phrases

Create a crazy phrase for each of the following groups of words. Groups of words that must remain in their current order are marked with an asterisk (*). You might even want to draw a simple picture to go along with each phrase.

| Group of Words | Crazy Phrase |
|---|---|
| **Rivers of Europe**<br>Po<br>Seine<br>Danube<br>Rhine<br>Rhone | **Partying Rats Sail Down Rivers.** |
| **Colonies in the Western Hemisphere, 1700**<br>Spanish<br>Portuguese<br>Dutch<br>French<br>English | |
| **Former Yugoslav States**<br>Slovenia<br>Croatia<br>Bosnia-Herzegovina<br>Serbia<br>Montenegro<br>Macedonia | |
| **The Terrestrial Planets**<br>*Mercury<br>*Venus<br>*Earth<br>*Mars | |
| **Atmosphere Layers**<br>*troposphere<br>*stratosphere<br>*mesosphere<br>*thermosphere<br>*exosphere | |

# **Memorizing and Remembering** *(cont.)*

## Pictures

Have you ever been stuck on a question while taking a test? You can almost remember the answer, but even banging your head on the desk will not jar it from your memory. What you need in a case like that is a picture. A picture, even a simple drawing, can give your brain that extra kick it needs to help you remember important information. Add a picture to the information you are studying, and later that picture can help you remember the information. The picture you make can be a simple doodle in the margin of your notes, or a detailed drawing which sums up the ideas in a chapter or a story. Take a look at the examples below.

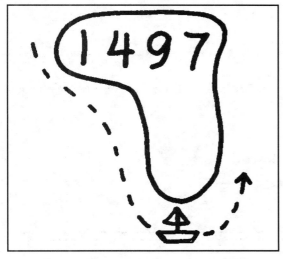

Vasco da Gama sailed around the southern tip of Africa in 1497.

Galileo used a telescope to prove the heliocentric theory (that the sun is in the center of the universe).

James Watt developed an improved steam engine in 1763.

Charlemagne was crowned emperor on Christmas Day in A.D. 800.

# **Memorizing and Remembering** *(cont.)*

## **Pictures** *(cont.)*

Pictures can also help you remember words.  For example, if you are studying the Ottoman Empire and you want to remember the name, think of it as auto-man, and draw a picture of a car (automobile) and a man.

In the example below, a picture is used to remember Kitty Hawk, North Carolina, the site of the Wright Brother's first flight (1903).

A detailed picture can help sum up the theme of a chapter you have been studying, like the picture below.  Add color, names, dates, and anything you want that will help you remember the information. You do not have to be an artist to make great pictures for studying.

Chapter 7: Ancient Egypt

# Memorizing and Remembering *(cont.)*

## Practice: Pictures

Draw a picture for each bit of information below. Focus on things in your drawings that will help you remember the information. Be creative with your ideas but try to keep your drawings simple and to the point. Too much detail can make it difficult to remember the important parts of the picture.

|  |  |
|---|---|
| A *cash crop* is a plant or plant product raised to make money. | *Enzymes* can build up or break down molecules. |
| At least 3,000 people were executed by *guillotine* during the *French Revolution* of the 1790s. | *England* defeated the *Spanish Armada* (fleet of warships) with smaller, faster ships (sailing ships). |
| A *fairy ring* is a circle of mushrooms in a grassy area. According to superstition, the circle is made by dancing fairies. | *Stalactites* are cone-shaped or cylinder-shaped deposits on the roofs of caves. They are the result of the dripping of mineral-rich water. |

# Memorizing and Remembering *(cont.)*

## Recordings

Another great way to memorize information is to listen to it. Use a cassette tape player to record information and play it back to yourself. Here are just some of the things you can record:

- Q & A notes
- vocabulary words and definitions
- spelling words
- reading assignments
- math formulas, theorems, and laws
- grammar rules
- facts, including dates of events
- summaries
- short stories and poems
- musical performance to critique

The most convenient thing about using a recording is that you can listen to it while you are doing something else, especially if you have a portable cassette player and headphones. You can listen to your recordings while you exercise, while you eat, while you ride in the car, or while you do chores. Here are a few helpful hints about making recordings:

1. Speak loudly and clearly when you are making a recording. Do not worry about sounding funny; everyone thinks his/her voice sounds strange on a recording, especially at first.

2. Label the recording. Start the recording with your name, the subject, the date, and other important information. Example "Testing. . . one, two, three. . . testing. This is a recording of Joan's spelling words, list number nine. Today is October tenth. The first word is. . . ."

3. Label the cassette tape. Use a general label if you are going to re-use the tape (e.g., *Fred's Study Tape*). Use a specific label if you are going to keep the tape as it is (e.g., *Fred's Chemical Reaction Tape*).

4. Be careful not to record over something you have already put on the tape. If you want to be sure something does not get recorded over accidentally, pop out the tabs on the top of the cassette. If you change your mind later and want to record on the cassette again, just cover each of the holes with a small piece of cellophane tape.

# Memorizing and Remembering *(cont.)*

## Unloading

Let's say you have memorized everything for the test. Your brain is packed full of information, and there are just a few things you are worried about forgetting. Here is what you do: When you get the test, turn it over and write down all the things you have memorized or at least the things you have worried about forgetting, such as acronyms, crazy phrases, spellings, pictures, formulas, dates, and names. This is called *unloading*. Once you have unloaded all the "heavy cargo," you will be able to relax and concentrate on the test questions.

You can *unload* any time during the test, too. Just be sure you are allowed to write on the test. If not, ask the teacher if you can use a piece of scratch paper to unload on.

## Quiz Me!

The only way to find out if you have really memorized the information you have been studying is to quiz yourself—that is, to ask yourself the questions and see if you can say the answers. Having other people quiz you on the information is fine, but other people are not always available. By using Q & A notes, flash cards, and recordings, you will be able to quiz yourself thoroughly. And remember, if you can't say it, you don't know it, so keep studying and quizzing yourself until you can say the answer again and again. Then you will know you have it memorized!

## How to Help the Quizzer

The quizzer, or the person who is quizzing you, has a very difficult job because he or she is probably unfamiliar with the information you are trying to learn. There are several things you can do to make the quizzer's job easier. First, be sure you are prepared to be quizzed. That is, be sure you have studied the information thoroughly before you ask someone to quiz you on it. Second, give the quizzer something to quiz you on, such as review questions, flash cards, question and answer notes, or a study guide. Third, tell the quizzer about the subject you are studying. Fourth, tell the quizzer what you have learned so far and what information you are still trying to master. Fifth, let the quizzer know how exact your answers must be. Depending upon the type of test you are studying for, you may or may not have to know the exact answer.

---

**Example:** Alex read through his question and answer notes one last time. He felt sure he had most of the information memorized when he asked his sister, Helga, to quiz him over his notes. Alex told his sister that the notes were over chemistry, which he had been studying in science. He explained that he had learned the information about physical and chemical changes, but that he was still working on the vocabulary definitions and the chemical formulas. He also explained that the questions from his notes that he had already mastered were marked with a check, and that she could skip those when she quizzed him. When Helga asked how exact his answers needed to be, Alex let her know that the definitions did not need to be exact because that part of the test was going to be matching, but that he needed to know the chemical formulas by heart.

---

# In a Word

Vocabulary is a part of every subject. When students become more proficient at studying vocabulary, they improve their study habits for all subjects. This chapter is designed to introduce students to several "tools" for studying vocabulary. Two general approaches to vocabulary are presented: studying for memorization and studying for recognition.

## Suggested Strategies and Activities

- Encourage your students to develop a routine for approaching and studying vocabulary, such as the method described on page 91, Getting to Know the Word.

- The Teach It method described on page 92 can be used with students in pairs or cooperative learning groups. Introduce a different word and definition to each cooperative learning group. Within their groups, have the students study the words and definitions. Then have your students break out of their cooperative learning groups and assemble into "teaching" groups, so that each member of the teaching group has a different word. Have each student teach his or her new word to the members of his or her teaching group.

- When introducing vocabulary as part of a lesson, let your students know the degree to which you expect them to know the definition. In other words, let them know whether they should study for memorization or recognition.

- Train your students in methods for memorizing definitions, such as using flash cards. Encourage them to vocalize the word and definition when studying.

- Train your students in methods for studying to recognize definitions, such as with matching cards.

- Have your students use the same size card and the same color ink or pencil for all their matching cards.

- If your students are using flash cards or matching cards, you may want them to accumulate the cards over the course of a unit or throughout the school year.

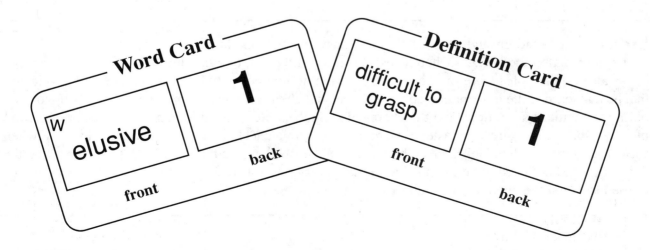

# In a Word *(cont.)*

If there is one thing you will have in just about every class, it is vocabulary. That is because when you study something new, you have to learn the terminology or the important words about the subject. Even video games come with instruction booklets that are packed full of new words. The one thing you do not want, however, is to have vocabulary take up too much of your study time. The methods in this chapter are designed to help you study vocabulary quickly and thoroughly so you can save time on homework, improve your vocabulary, and make better test scores.

## Getting to Know the Word

The first thing to do with vocabulary is to get to know the new words. Follow the steps below.

1. Read the word as it is used in the textbook or the story. Read the entire sentence and the sentences around it. This should give you a pretty good idea of what the word means.

2. Read the definition from the glossary in the back of the book. If a glossary is not available, use a dictionary.

3. Neatly copy the word and its definition on loose-leaf paper. If you find that the word has more than one definition and you are not sure which one to use, check with your teacher. Be sure to label the paper.

4. Underline the key word or words in the definition. These are the words that are unique or most important to the definition. Take a look at the example on the next page. If you are not sure which words are the key words, ask your teacher.

5. As you study the vocabulary word, focus on the key word(s) in the definition.

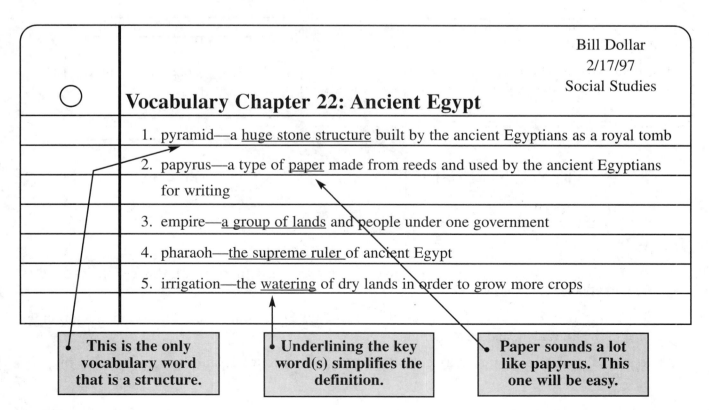

Bill Dollar
2/17/97
Social Studies

**Vocabulary Chapter 22: Ancient Egypt**

1. pyramid—a <u>huge stone structure</u> built by the ancient Egyptians as a royal tomb

2. papyrus—a type of <u>paper</u> made from reeds and used by the ancient Egyptians for writing

3. empire—<u>a group of lands</u> and people under one government

4. pharaoh—<u>the supreme ruler</u> of ancient Egypt

5. irrigation—the <u>watering</u> of dry lands in order to grow more crops

| **This is the only vocabulary word that is a structure.** | **Underlining the key word(s) simplifies the definition.** | **Paper sounds a lot like papyrus. This one will be easy.** |

# In a Word *(cont.)*

## Memorizing Definitions

You do not have to memorize the definition of a word to be able to use it. But if you are having a vocabulary test, you might need to know the definition by heart.

One of the best ways to memorize vocabulary definitions is to use flash cards. Flash cards are explained on pages 78 and 79. In addition to using flash cards, try the word of the day method, and the teach-it method. Both methods are very effective and take very little time.

## Word of the Day

1. At the beginning of each day choose a vocabulary word to be the word of the day.

2. In the morning make a flash card for that word (if you have not already done so) and try to memorize the definition.

3. Take the flash card with you to school and study it now and then. By the end of the day you will have it memorized. Take a look at page 78 for information on how to make and use flash cards.

### Good Times for Studying Flash Cards

- waiting for the bus

- eating lunch

- riding the bus

- before school

- waiting in the lunch line

- between classes

## Teach It

1. Teach at least three other people the word of the day and its definition. Choose people who are not already studying that word.

2. Teach the word at three different times during the day. For example, teach it once in the morning, once in the afternoon, and once at night.

3. Try to get each person to memorize the definition, and try to teach him or her without looking at your flash card.

# In a Word *(cont.)*

## Vocabulary Matching Tests

If your vocabulary test is going to be a matching test, then you really will not need to memorize the definitions. You will only have to know each definition well enough to match it to the correct word. The methods described below can help you study vocabulary words for a matching test. Two of the methods involve using flash cards. To find out how to make and use flash cards, see pages 78 and 79.

**Flash Card Method 1:** Make flash cards for each vocabulary word. Underline the key word or words in the definition on the back of the card (answer side). Study the words using the flash cards, but all you will need to do to get the answer right is say the key word or words.

**Flash Card Method 2:** Do the same as method 1, except put only the key word or words on the back of the card (answer side).

**Matching Cards:** Study the vocabulary definitions by using matching cards. Follow the steps below.

1. In large letters, write the vocabulary word on an index card. Label the same side of the card with a **W** (for word) in the upper left corner. Write a large number 1 on the back.

2. Write the definition of the vocabulary word on a separate card, again using large letters. Label the same side of the card with a **D** (for definition) in the upper left corner. Write a large number 1 on the back.

3. Repeat steps one and two for each vocabulary word on your list, numbering each pair consecutively. That is, the next pair should be number 2, and the next pair number 3, and so on.

4. Separate the cards into two groups: words and definitions. Practice matching each word to its definition, or vice versa. Select the word card and definition card that you think go together. Flip the pair of cards over to see if they have the same number. When you successfully match a pair of cards, remove that pair from the game.

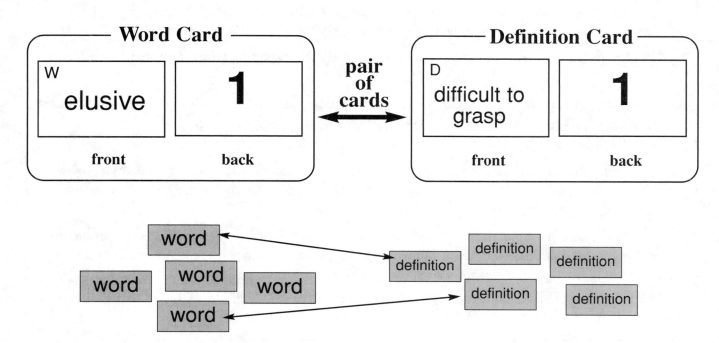

# Spell It!

How is spelling like playing the piano?  Perhaps one similarity is that both skills are more easily developed at a young age.  The point is that students are in their prime for becoming good spellers.  That is, the school age years present the best opportunity for developing a repertoire of words that the student can confidently spell correctly.

This chapter presents a variety of activities for studying spelling words.  It is suggested that these activities be presented in conjunction with lessons covering basic spelling rules.

## Suggested Strategies and Activities

- Have each of your students make a personal spelling list to keep track of frequently misspelled words.

- Have your students practice their words using one or more of the activities presented in this chapter.  You may want to give each student a copy of the Personal Spelling List form.  This form is located in the appendix.

- Have your class create a consolidated list of words from their personal spelling lists.  Ask each student to "donate" one or two of their words to the group list.  You may want to use the group list as an assigned spelling list for the class.

- When grading a student's assignment, mark any recurring misspelled words with a special abbreviation or symbol that indicates that it should be placed on his or her personal spelling list.

- Give your students a list of ten spelling words each week.  Have them work through the spelling activities from pages 96 and 97 to practice spelling the words.  You may want to let them choose five of the seven activities.

- If you assign a weekly spelling list, consider giving a pretest over the words.  This will allow your students to see which words they should focus on as they study.  You may want to have your students complete spelling activities exclusively for the words they misspell on the pretest.

- Encourage your students to create new ways to study their spelling words and share their ideas with the class.

- Emphasize to your students the importance of practicing the correct spelling of the words.  Offer the analogy of a professional musician or athlete who practices incorrectly.  Ask your students what they think might happen during the performance.

- Train your students in finding spelling mistakes.  Give them a paragraph to edit that has misspelled words from their assigned list or personal spelling lists.  This can also be done in cooperative learning groups.

- Play "spellball" with the class.  One student tosses a ball to a classmate and calls out a random spelling word from the assigned spelling list.  The second student must catch the ball and spell the word correctly or he or she is out.  Play continues until there is only one student left.  You may want to clarify that the ball must be tossed relatively softly and on target.  If the ball is not "catchable" then the student throwing the ball is out.

# **Spell It!** *(cont.)*

Spelling is everywhere. It is in all your classes, even math, and it is a big part of studying, too. If you are good at spelling, then you are in great shape and will save quite a bit of time studying and editing your assignments. If your spelling needs improvement, you will be glad to know that it is a skill which you can improve with practice. In this chapter we will look at several ways to study and practice spelling words, including personal spelling lists, writing activities, flash cards, and recordings.

## Personal Spelling List

One of the most frustrating things about spelling is misspelling the same word again and again. To avoid this, use a personal spelling list to keep track of the words you tend to misspell. It is easy to do. Follow the steps below.

1. Label a piece of loose-leaf paper and title it "Personal Spelling List" or use a copy of the Personal Spelling List form in the appendix in the back of this book.

2. Each time you misspell a word (except for careless mistakes) write it on your personal spelling list.

3. Take a few minutes each day during your study session to review the words on your list. You can use flash cards, recordings, or writing activities to help you study the words.

4. When you feel you have mastered a word—that is, you are no longer misspelling it—check it off your list.

*Wendy Waters*
*9/10/95*
*Spelling*

*Personal Spelling List*

✔ 1. *believe*
✔ 2. *probably*
3. *chocolate*
4. *favorite*
5. *become*

# Spell It! *(cont.)*

## Spelling Activities

Many students practice their spelling words by writing them over and over.  Listed below are some interesting activities that involve writing your spelling words.  Let's take a look at these activities as they are used with a list of five words: *believe, probably, chocolate, favorite, become.*

1. **Alphabetize the words.**

   - become
   - believe
   - chocolate
   - favorite
   - probably

2. **Categorize the words by syllables.**

   **_Two Syllables_**     **_Three Syllables_**

   - become              - chocolate
   - believe              - favorite
                          - probably

3. **List the words from shortest to longest by number of letters.**

   - become
   - believe
   - favorite
   - probably
   - chocolate

4. **Combine the words into one meaningful sentence.**  (If your list has more than five words, combine any five into one meaningful sentence.)

   I *believe chocolate* will *probably become* my *favorite* flavor.

5. **List the words in pyramid form from easiest to hardest.**  The word at the top should be the one that is the easiest for you to spell.  The word at the bottom should be the one that is the hardest for you to spell.

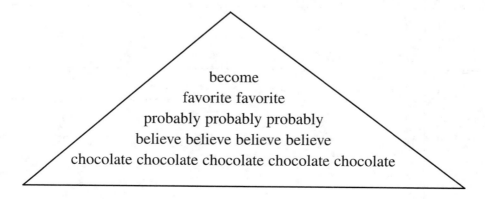

become
favorite favorite
probably probably probably
believe believe believe believe
chocolate chocolate chocolate chocolate chocolate

# Spell It! *(cont.)*

## Spelling Activities *(cont.)*

6. Make a game with the words, such as a word search or a crossword puzzle. Using graph paper makes this even easier. Complete the activity by playing the game.

**Word Search**

- chocolate
- become
- believe
- favorite
- probably

| c | h | b | e | c | o | m | e | v | u |
|---|---|---|---|---|---|---|---|---|---|
| y | d | m | u | h | k | w | t | j | h |
| e | l | a | r | z | n | p | i | m | y |
| n | b | b | j | q | y | k | r | z | g |
| r | e | t | a | l | o | c | o | h | c |
| f | l | r | g | b | r | h | v | l | o |
| x | s | w | u | t | o | m | a | b | n |
| n | p | i | w | s | a | r | f | a | k |
| u | q | y | h | f | s | q | p | l | i |
| b | e | l | i | e | v | e | k | r | v |

7. Draw a picture using spelling words.

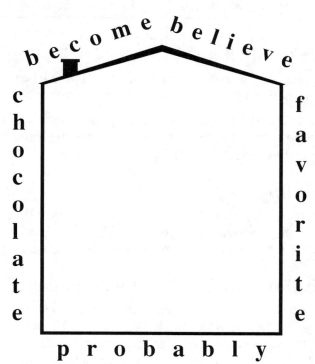

# Spell It! *(cont.)*

## Spelling Flash Cards

Follow the steps below to make and study spelling flash cards. Take a look at the example below.

1. On the front of an index card, draw a picture or a symbol which tells you what the word is.

2. Write the spelling word on the back of the card. Be sure to spell it correctly.

3. On the front of the card, along with the picture, you may want to add the first letter of the word and the total number of letters in the word as clues.

4. To study the spelling words, follow steps 3 through 7 on pages 78 and 79, except that the question side of the card will be your picture, and the answer side will be your spelling word.

5. If you get an answer wrong, write the word three times on a piece of scratch paper. Then say the word and spell it two times.

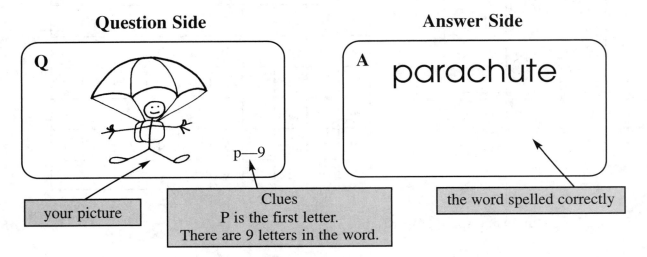

## Recordings For Spelling

In most spelling tests, the words are announced by the teacher and written by the students. To study the same way, have someone say the words to you while you write the correct spelling for each.

You can also use a recording to practice your spelling words. Using a cassette player, record yourself saying each spelling word. Pause long enough between words to give yourself a chance to write. Then play back the recording and try to spell each word correctly.

## Sandbox Spelling

Fill a small container, such as a shoebox, with clean sand. Practice your spelling words by tracing the letters in the sand. Say the letters as you trace them. This will allow you to hear and feel the spelling of the words. After you finish one word, smooth out the sand and trace the next word.

## Word of the Day and Teach It for Spelling

You can use the word of the day and teach-it methods to study spelling words. Both methods are described on page 92 for use with vocabulary words. However, instead of a vocabulary word, make it a spelling word of the day. Instead of teaching others the definition of the word, quiz them on the spelling of the word. If they misspell the word, teach them the correct spelling.

# Using Charts

During school students are exposed to a large number and variety of charts. However, few students use charts as study tools. This chapter is designed to help students realize the potential charts have when it comes to studying. Four basic types of charts are presented. Given the great variety of charts available, you may want to add additional charts to the ones presented, especially those that you use regularly in your lessons. Focus your students on the potential these charts have for their own individual use, such as in taking notes, reviewing for a test, or adding a visual to a report or presentation.

## Suggested Strategies and Activities

- Have your students complete the practice activity on page 102. To extend this activity, have your students create other types of charts for the same article. This can be done in cooperative learning groups, with each group creating a different chart. Each type of chart can serve a different purpose, representing a different aspect of the article. That is, each chart need not focus on the same information from the article.

- Lead your students in a class discussion concerning the strengths and weaknesses of each type of chart. Draw conclusions as to the most appropriate uses for each chart. This can be done in conjunction with the extended activity mentioned above.

- Gather statistical information about the students in your class, such as gender, age, eye color, number of pets, favorite color, siblings, etc. Write this information on the chalkboard in a random fashion. Working in groups, have one half the students compile the information into a paragraph, and the other half create a chart which organizes the information. This activity can serve to demonstrate the usefulness of charts.

- The variety of charts which your students can use for studying is practically endless. Encourage your students to design their own customized charts when they study.

- When giving a writing assignment or an essay test, offer bonus points for including a relevant, well-made chart.

- As an end-of-the-year review project, have each of your students illustrate, in the form of a chart, the major ideas or other important information, from one of the units or chapters you have covered in your subject area.

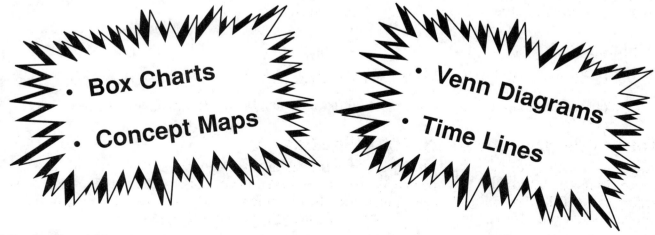

- Box Charts
- Concept Maps
- Venn Diagrams
- Time Lines

# Using Charts *(cont.)*

A chart is an excellent tool for studying. Charts make it possible to organize a lot of information in a small area. You can use charts to organize information for a writing assignment, to organize ideas while you are brainstorming, or to plan out the steps for solving a math problem. A chart can also be an excellent addition to a report, an essay, or a project. In this chapter we will take a look at several different types of charts, including box charts, compare-and-contrast charts, concept maps, and time lines.

## Box Charts

A box chart can help you organize information into different categories. The box chart below organizes important information about three different types of joints in the human body.

| Type of Joint | Motion | Location |
|---|---|---|
| hinged | back and forth | elbow and knee |
| sliding | sliding | wrist and ankle |
| ball and socket | circular | shoulder and hip |

## Compare-and-Contrast Charts

Compare-and-contrast charts help to organize the similarities and differences between two subjects. The chart below is a special kind of compare-and-contrast chart called a Venn diagram. It organizes some similarities and differences between the planets Venus and Mars.

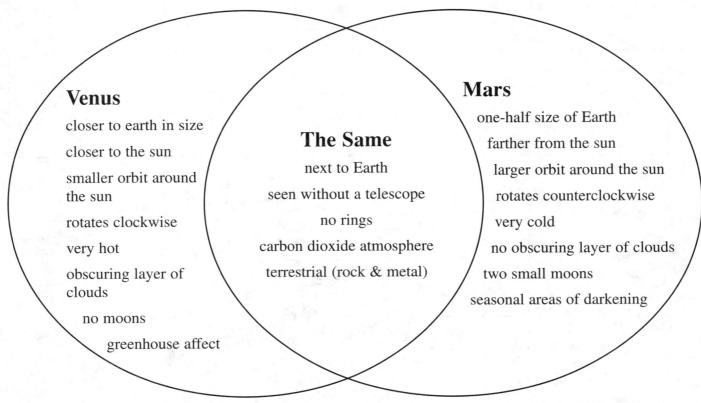

**Venus**
- closer to earth in size
- closer to the sun
- smaller orbit around the sun
- rotates clockwise
- very hot
- obscuring layer of clouds
- no moons
- greenhouse affect

**The Same**
- next to Earth
- seen without a telescope
- no rings
- carbon dioxide atmosphere
- terrestrial (rock & metal)

**Mars**
- one-half size of Earth
- farther from the sun
- larger orbit around the sun
- rotates counterclockwise
- very cold
- no obscuring layer of clouds
- two small moons
- seasonal areas of darkening

# Using Charts *(cont.)*

## Concept Maps

To organize ideas and their details, use a concept map. Concept maps are great for showing how different ideas are connected. Start at the top with the main idea or concept and branch out to other ideas and details that are related. The ideas and details from a unit, chapter, lesson, or story can be organized with a concept map.

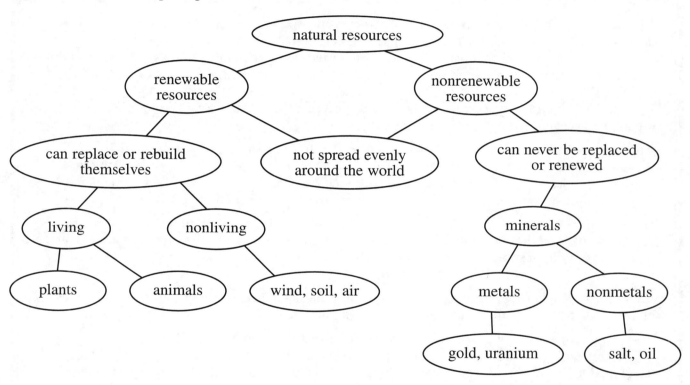

## Time Lines

Time lines are useful for organizing information related to events and their dates. Time lines show the order of events and how much time has passed between events. Time lines can be either vertical or horizontal. The vertical time line below shows events related to the rise and fall of the Egyptian empire.

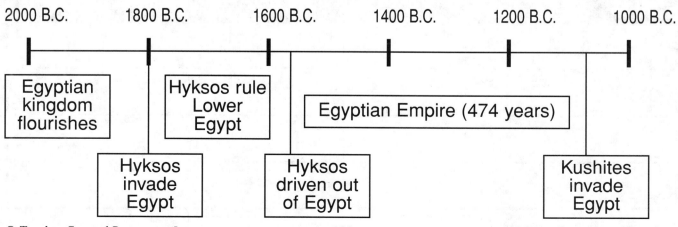

# Using Charts *(cont.)*

## Practice: Using Charts

Use the chart below to organize important information from the article.

### Digging into Our Past

Archaeologists literally dig up the past. They carefully excavate a site inch-by-inch in their never-ending search for artifacts that will provide clues to civilizations of long ago. It wasn't until the 1700's, though, that people became interested in studying old cultures. When gold or any other valuable object was found, it was kept by the finder; other artifacts were discarded. Then in 1748 a farmer in a Italy unearthed an underground wall while he was digging in a field. He had discovered Pompeii, which had been destroyed by a volcano some 1,700 years earlier. An organized excavation uncovered these ancient ruins.

Another big find occurred in 1799. A French soldier found a stone tablet near the town of Rosetta, Egypt. This stone contained the same message in hieroglyphics, Egyptian demotic writing, and Greek. French archeologist Jean Francis Champollion studied the writings on the Rosetta Stone and was able to figure out the hieroglyphs by translating the Greek.

During the late 1800's Sir Flinders Petrie began working in Egypt. He studied everything he found and worked inch by inch. His meticulous methods paid off. He found pottery, tools, and other everyday items used by the Egyptians. Because of his careful and methodical work, Petrie is called "The Father of Modern Archaeology."

In the early 1900's Howard Carter began searching for an ancient tomb in Egypt. Finally in 1922 he found King Tut's (King Tutankhamen) tomb and mummy.

Many other amazing discoveries about our ancient heritage have been made in the last century. Today archaeologists are busy at work in places such as Pompeii and the Red Sea. Specially developed tools and newly developed methods such as radio-carbon dating help them determine more accurately the origin of artifacts. Perhaps you would like to become an archaeologist to help our human race learn more about its past.

From TCM's "Digging into Our Past," page 71, #292 *Thematic Unit—Ancient Egypt.*

| Date | Location of Excavation | Person or Archaeologist | Artifact Discovered | Importance of Discovery |
|---|---|---|---|---|
|  |  |  |  |  |
|  |  |  |  |  |
|  |  |  |  |  |
|  |  |  |  |  |

# Quick Writing

The writing process can be a very effective tool for students. However, many students ignore the writing process completely when the assignment they are working on does not call for multiple drafts. And often, students are not afforded time to create several drafts of their work, such as when they are doing essay tests or in-class writing activities. Yet, there are important elements in the writing process that can be applied to these limited-time assignments. In this chapter, this is referred to as *quick writing*.

Quick writing is a method which applies the writing process as a study skill. The purpose of quick writing is to encourage students to reflect on their writing, even when they are not planning a second draft. In essence, quick writing is the writing process streamlined for one-draft assignments. It involves brainstorming, organizing ideas, writing, and proofreading, and it can be applied to simple review questions or a full-length essay.

## Suggested Strategies and Activities

Charts can be very helpful for organizing ideas. You may want to cover pages 99 through 102 with your students before completing this chapter.

- Two practice activities are discussed in this chapter, one for proofreading and one for organizing information. Both activities can be completed with cooperative learning groups.

- Have your students follow the steps for quick writing for a short essay on a subject they are most interested in, such as a sport, hobby, or favorite musician. Time each step of the process: five minutes for brainstorming, ten minutes for organizing, fifteen minutes for writing, and ten minutes for proofreading.

- Review standard editing marks and procedures with your students. Demonstrate how these may be applied in the proofreading activity on page 106.

- Post the quick writing steps in your classroom. Remind your students to apply these steps to all of their one-draft writing activities. In addition, emphasize the importance of redrafting an assignment when the proofreading steps result in a heavily marked corrected paper.

- Remind your students that quick writing is not sufficient for reports, projects, and other writing assignments that involve more time. These assignments should see several drafts and result in a highly polished product.

1. Brainstorm.
2. Organize your ideas.
3. Write your answer.
4. Proofread.

# Quick Writing *(cont.)*

If you have ever used the writing process, you know that it involves a step-by-step method for writing. When you use the writing process, you write a rough draft and revise and rewrite it several times until you have a final draft. This is the best way to create a final, perfected writing assignment. However, for some writing assignments, such as answering an essay question on a test, or writing a paragraph as a quick activity during class, there is not enough time for writing and revising several drafts.

For limited-time or one-draft, assignments there are many steps in the writing process that can still be very helpful. In this chapter, we will look at ways to use these steps through a system called *quick writing*. The four simple steps for quick writing are explained below and on the next page. As you will see, quick writing involves brainstorming ideas, organizing those ideas, writing an answer, and proofreading the answer. To keep things simple, as we go through a the quick-writing steps, we will refer to the writing assignment as an answer.

1. **Brainstorm.**

   Brainstorm a list of ideas and create an idea bank. To do this, write down everything you can think about the subject in a special area on your paper or scratch paper. This area will be your idea bank. It is important to write these ideas down so that you do not forget them while you are writing your answer. Do not pass up any ideas, even if at first you think they are not good ones. Sometimes a not-so-good idea can lead to a better one. These ideas can be words, phrases, sentences, dates, symbols, acronyms, or anything else related to the subject. If you are having trouble coming up with ideas, try these things:

   - Talk through the ideas you already have or illustrate them.

   - Ask yourself questions about the ideas you already have.

   - Think of the activities you did with your class when learning about the subject.

   - Focus on any special words you have been studying in your class, such as vocabulary related to the subject.

   - If you are allowed, try to get some ideas from other sources, such as your textbook or your notes.

**Writing Assignment:** Compare and contrast renewable and nonrenewable resources.

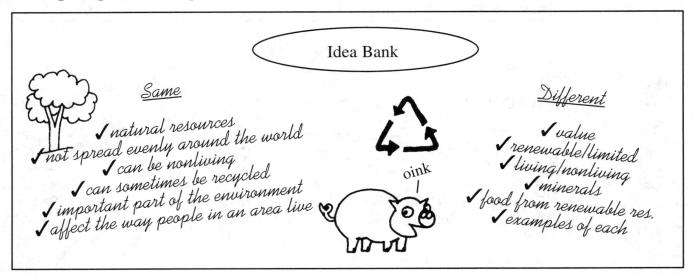

# Quick Writing *(cont.)*

2. **Organize your ideas.**

   Choose ideas from your idea bank that you want to include in your answer. It is not always necessary to use all the ideas in your idea bank. Put these ideas in the order in which you want them to appear in your answer. You can use a chart, an outline, or a list to organize your ideas. In the example below, a chart is used to organize the similarities and differences between renewable and nonrenewable resources.

   *Differences*

   *Similarities*

   *Differences*

   - Renewable
   - can be renewed or replaced if used correctly
   - lesser value because replenished
   - living and nonliving
   - more often a source of foods
   - wind, water, plants, animals, sunlight

   - natural resources
   - not spread evenly around the world
   - important part of the environment
   - affect the way people live in an area
   - can sometimes be recycled
   - can be nonliving material

   - Nonrenewable
   - can never be replaced or renewed once used
   - higher value because of limited supply
   - only nonliving material
   - more often a source of energy
   - salt, cool, oil, metals, natural gas

3. **Write your answer.**

   When writing your answer, use your best handwriting and write double spaced or every other line if you can. This will make it easier to edit your work when you proofread. Work from your outline or whatever you have used to organize your ideas but feel free to add additional details, such as dates and examples that are not included in your outline. The example on the next page is made up of two paragraphs. The first paragraph is about the similarities between renewable and nonrenewable resources, and the second paragraph is about the differences.

4. **Proofread your answer.**

   Check your answer for errors in spelling, capitalization, punctuation, and grammar, and make any corrections as neatly as possible. Check for run-on sentences and be sure to indent each paragraph. Most importantly, however, make sure that your answer makes sense as you read it. If it does not make sense to you, then it will definitely confuse the reader.

Read through your answer aloud. This is important because your eyes can actually play tricks on you and see things incorrectly. Your ears, however, will accurately hear the words you say. By reading the words aloud, you are much more likely to notice mistakes. If you are in a situation where you cannot read aloud, then read your answer aloud in your mind. That is, hear yourself say each word in your mind as if you were speaking.

# Quick Writing *(cont.)*

## Practice: Proofreading

The writing assignment below was written as an answer to an essay question on a test. Before it can be turned in, it must be taken through the fourth step in the quick writing process. Proofread the answer for any mistakes in grammar, spelling, punctuation, or capitalization. Correct any mistakes as neatly as possible.

---

*Test Question:*

*Compare and contrast renewable and nonrenewable resources.*

Renewable and Nonrenewable resources have many things in common. Both are natural resources which are not spread evenly around the world. Both renewable ad nonrenewable resources are an important part of the environment and greatly affect the way people live in an area. Another similarity is that some renewable resources, such as water, and some nonrenewable resources, such as metals, can be recycled.

However, there are also many differences between renewable and nonrenewable resources. Nonrenewable resources are often more valuable because they can never be replaced or renewed. Renewable resources can replace or rebuild themselves. as long as they are used wisely, renewable resources will always bee available. Nonrenewable resources are made up of non-living material and are often a source of energy. Renewable resources can be of living or non-living material and our often a source of food. examples of renewable resources include plants, animals, sunlight, wind, soil. Examples of nonrenewable resources include salt, cool, oil, and naturals gas.

---

# Quick Writing *(cont.)*

## Other Tips About Writing

✔ When possible, it is always best to complete the full writing process. The full writing process involves several more drafts, additional brainstorming, having your answer critiqued by another person, and creating a final, polished answer.

✔ Keep track of editing marks or corrections that your teacher makes on your graded papers, such as spelling errors or run-on sentences. These are the things you should look for most when you proofread your work. Add any frequently misspelled words to your personal spelling list. You may want to create a personal proofreading list to keep track of other errors. The personal spelling list is covered on page 95.

✔ Another important step in the proofreading process is to check to be sure that you have labeled your paper completely.

✔ One of the best ways to improve your writing is to read more often. Reading will help all areas of your writing, including spelling, punctuation, grammar, and vocabulary. In a way, your brain actually studies these things as you read, even if you are not aware of it, and even if you are reading about an exciting subject.

✔ Keep in mind the importance of good handwriting. A neatly written answer will have a better chance of receiving a higher grade.

✔ There may be times when you feel you do not have time even for the quick writing steps. For example, you may find yourself running out of time on a test, and you have not started the essay question at the end. In cases like this, try to go through the quick writing steps in your mind, if not on paper. And, most importantly, be sure to proofread your answer.

✔ When the writing assignment involves answering a question, be sure to restate the question in your answer. This will help make your answer clear. A restated question also makes an excellent topic sentence for a paragraph.

    Example:

    Q—What is a *polis?*

    A—A polis is a Greek city-state.

# This Is a Test!

Students can benefit greatly from training in a structured approach to testing. Such training can help them develop a collection of strategies for test taking and preparation. When students become aware of these strategies and are trained in how to apply them, they become more sensitive to the cause-and-effect relationship between preparation and performance in testing. In addition to improving scores, such training can boost confidence and reduce test anxiety.

The strategies presented in this chapter are designed to enlighten students as to the nature of tests and how to prepare for them and take them more effectively. Included are strategies for taking and preparing for tests of different types or formats, such as matching or essay. In this chapter, tests are categorized into two characteristic groups: recognition tests where you get to choose the answer, such as in multiple choice; and recall tests where you have to produce the answer, such as fill-in-the-blank or completion types.

## Suggested Strategies and Activities

- Have your students brainstorm a list of questions that a student might want to ask about an upcoming test. Then, have your students compare their lists with the one on page 109.

- Acquire old tests of different types—true/false, short answer, etc. Have students use them to practice strategies for taking different types of tests. You can also use these old tests to introduce study strategies for different types of tests.

- If possible, allow your students to write on the test you are administering. Train them in strategies for circling important information in directions and test items. Also, train them in techniques for jotting down important information at the beginning of a test. This is described as *unloading* on page 89.

- Introduce your students to recognition and recall tests by giving them two short, mock tests over the same material, one recognition and one recall. Ask your students to compare and contrast the two tests and the preparation requirements for each.

- In cooperative learning groups, have your students develop different question types, such as multiple choice, fill-in-the-blank, true/false, and essay for the same bit of information, such as a current event. Have each group of students share their questions with the class.

- Test your students in a variety of formats, such as matching, essay, multiple choice, open-book, or open-note. Use this opportunity to introduce specific study strategies for different types of tests. Help your students develop review activities that are appropriate for the type of test being given. Also, coach your students on strategies for taking these different types of tests.

- At the beginning of a unit, advise your students of the type of test that will be given when the unit is completed. This will allow them to gear their study strategies to a test of that type.

# This Is a Test! *(cont.)*

Imagine that you have a good friend who is an engineer, and she has just designed and built a new type of aircraft called the *Turbo-warp*. She offers to take you for a ride on her first flight. Would you go? If you answered "yes," then you are either a real dare-devil or you have forgotten about test flights. It would not be wise to fly in the Turbo-warp until it had been thoroughly tested. You see, testing is an important part of life, especially for people in school. Tests help us to measure ability, potential, and growth.

Did you know that there are strategies that you can use to improve your test-taking skills? In this chapter we will focus on those strategies that can help you study for tests and take tests more effectively.

## Get the Whole Story

The more you know about a test, the better you will do. Listed below are some important questions to ask the teacher about an upcoming test.

| Questions to Ask | Reason for the Question |
|---|---|
| 1. Will this be a test or a quiz? | • This will let you how important it is. A quiz is usually a smaller part of your grade than a test. |
| 2. When will the test be? | • This lets you know how much time you have to prepare for the test. |
| 3. What type of test will it be (true/false, multiple choice, matching, fill-in-the-blank, essay)? | • This will tell you how to study for the test. |
| 4. Will there be a review in class? | • Teachers often have a review for the test in class or a special study session before or after school. |
| 5. Will there be a study guide or a review worksheet for the test? | • A study guide or a review worksheet can be a big help when you are preparing for a test. |
| 6. Will this be an open-book test? | • On open-book tests, you can use your textbook and sometimes your notes to help answer questions. |
| 7. Will there be any questions about information from the lecture that is not in the book? | • Sometimes the teacher will talk to the class about ideas that the textbook does not cover. Find out what that information is and be sure that you have it in your notes. |
| 8. How much time will be given to finish the test? | • This will let you know how fast you will have to work. |

# This Is a Test! *(cont.)*

## Taking the Test

Now it is time to take the test. First, let's look at some things you can do before the test begins to help you to get ready. Then we will go over some test-taking strategies you can use during the test which can help improve your score.

## Before the Test

1. Sit down right away and take a few minutes to review one last time for the test. If you have any information you want to remember for unloading (see page 89), then look that over now.

2. Follow the testing procedure that your teacher requires, such as clearing your desk, using a cover sheet, or using a number two pencil.

3. Ask any last minute questions about the information you have studied or about the directions for the test.

4. Listen carefully to any instructions given by the teacher.

5. When you get your test, read the directions very carefully and circle or underline any important parts, unless you are not allowed to write on the test.

> **Test Directions:** Match each vocabulary word with a definition. Use each vocabulary word only once.

## During the Test

1. Label every part of the test, except any parts you are not supposed to write on. Remember, the most important part of the label is your name.

2. Answer all the questions. Do not spend too much time on any one question. If you get stuck on a question, then take a guess and mark that question with a check.

3. You do not always have to start at the beginning of the test. If the test is made up of different sections, begin with the section that you want to get out of the way first. You may find it helpful to complete essay or short-answer sections first.

4. When you have finished answering all the questions, go back and review those questions that you answered with guesses. Change an answer only if you are sure it is wrong. When you feel comfortable with your answer, erase the check mark.

5. If there is a time limit to finish the test, then you will want to keep a close eye on the clock. You may also want to request that your teacher make an announcement when one-half the time is up and when there are only two minutes left. If time is almost up and you have not finished, ask your teacher for extra time.

6. Before you hand in your test, go back and double check each answer. Change an answer only if you are reasonably sure it is wrong.

7. Use information in the test questions and answers as a source or a place to get information. You might even find the answer to one question somewhere else on the test. When you are writing an essay answer and you are unsure about the spelling of an important word, see if you can find that word printed somewhere else in the test. Take a look at the examples on the next page.

# This Is a Test! *(cont.)*

## During the Test *(cont.)*

Question 9 actually tells you the answer to question 7: the *Nile River.*

### Egypt Test page 2

7. What is the name of the river that runs through Egypt?
   a. the Mississippi
   b. the Nile
   c. the African

8. The writing system used by the ancient Egyptians is called _____ .
   a. hieroglyphics
   b. the alphabet
   c. cuneiform

9. The ancient Egyptians used the Nile River to _____ their crops.
   a. flood
   b. harvest
   c. irrigate

10. Which class was at the bottom of the social pyramid?
    a. government officials
    b. musicians
    c. slaves

Use information from question 10 to help answer the essay question: *Egyptian society was organized by classes into a social pyramid.*

### Egypt Test page 3

Short Answer Essay

1. How was ancient Egyptian society organized?

# This Is a Test! *(cont.)*

## Strategies for Taking Different Types of Tests

## Matching

1. Read through the directions carefully. Find out whether or not the answers can be used more than once.

2. If you have to match letters to numbers as in the example below, then use capital letters and make them clear and simple.

3. Look for key words in the questions, such as those circled in the example.

4. Do not cross out answers as you use them unless you are absolutely sure they are correct. If you are not sure, then put a check by the answer instead.

> **Example:** On the matching quiz below, suppose you choose *Acropolis* for number 1. Since you are not sure this is correct, you put a check by *Acropolis*, answer c. Later, when you read question 6, you realize that *Acropolis* is the correct answer for number 6 and you make the change. If you had crossed out *Acropolis*, you might not have considered it a possible answer for one of the other questions.

---

### Vocabulary Quiz

**Questions**

1. __E__    A city-state in ancient Greece.

2. __F__    Land that is surrounded by water on three sides.

3. __A__    The central marketplace in ancient Athens.

4. __D__    A territory that is under the control of another country.

5. __B__    A person captured by Sparta and forced to live as slave.

6. __C__    A hilltop fortress in ancient Athens which included the Parthenon and other famous buildings.

**Answers**

   a.  agora

   b.  helot

✔  c.  Acropolis

   d.  colony

   e.  polis

   f.  peninsula

⬭ **= Key Words**

---

# This Is a Test! (cont.)

## Strategies for Taking Different Types of Tests (cont.)

## Multiple Choice

1. Read the directions carefully. Find out whether or not you may choose more than one answer per question.

2. Read the question and each answer choice carefully. Look for the *best* answer. If two or more of the answer choices seem correct, then you must decide which one is the *most* correct.

3. If you are allowed to write on the test, then circle or underline important words in the question.

> **Example:**
> Which of these **is not** a chemical change?
> (a.) ice melting
> b. wood burning
> c. metal rusting
> d. a battery making electricity

4. Suspect the larger, more detailed answers as being correct.

5. Strongly suspect "all of the above" as the correct answer. If you are sure that at least two of the answer choices are correct, then go with "all of the above."

6. If you are not sure which answer to choose, then use the process of elimination. Start by crossing out answers you are *sure* are wrong. Then cross out answers you think are *probably* wrong. The more you narrow down your choices, the better your chances are of choosing the correct answer.

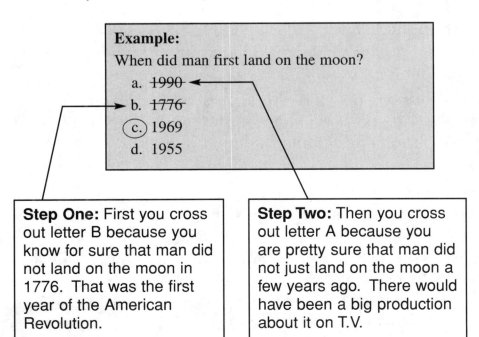

> **Example:**
> When did man first land on the moon?
> a. ~~1990~~
> b. ~~1776~~
> (c.) 1969
> d. 1955

**Step One:** First you cross out letter B because you know for sure that man did not land on the moon in 1776. That was the first year of the American Revolution.

**Step Two:** Then you cross out letter A because you are pretty sure that man did not just land on the moon a few years ago. There would have been a big production about it on T.V.

**Step Three:** Now that you have eliminated answers A and B, you can concentrate on the two answers you suspect are correct: C and D. You know that man first landed on the moon during this century, and you think it was during the 1960's. You choose answer C, 1969, which is correct.

# This Is a Test! *(cont.)*

## True or False

1. Read the statement very carefully.

2. If any part of the statement is false, then the whole thing is false. In statement A below, it is true that there are many young teachers, but not every single one has a funny haircut.

3. Look out for absolutes such as *always, never, every, only*, and *all*. They often indicate a false statement. In statement B, you cannot say that math teachers *always* give too much homework because there are days when they give no homework at all.

4. More flexible words such as *usually, generally, sometimes, frequently*, and *occasionally* often indicate a true statement, as in statement C.

5. Look out for the word *because*. Many times *because* is used to link two true statements together in a way that makes the whole thing false, as in statement D. School can be fun but *not* because some teachers love coffee.

6. Longer statements are usually correct, like statement E.

7. If you are given the option, write out the words *true* and *false*. If you have to use the letters T and F, be sure to write them very clearly.

---

**Example:**

**True or False?**

  A. Many teachers are young, and they all have funny haircuts.

  B. Math teachers always give too much homework.

  C. Teachers are occasionally nice, frequently strict, and sometimes cool.

  D. School can be fun because some teachers love to drink coffee.

  E. In 1450 Johann Gutenberg developed a printing press with moveable type which greatly affected the spread of the Protestant Reformation.

---

## Fill-in-the-Blank

1. Look to see if all of the blanks are the same size. If they are not, then ask your teacher if the size of a blank indicates the size of the answer. Also, ask whether or not there can be more than one word per blank, or if each blank is for a separate word.

2. Read the statement carefully.

3. Write your answer very neatly.

4. Your answer will have to be exact. If you are unsure about the spelling of a word, look to see if that word is printed somewhere else on the test.

5. Be sure that your answer is grammatically correct. If your answer sounds awkward and does not seem to fit into the sentence correctly, then it is probably not the correct answer.

6. If all else fails, then be sure to guess. If you leave the blank empty, then it will definitely be marked wrong. But if you guess, your answer just might be correct.

# This Is a Test! *(cont.)*

## Fill-In-The-Blank *(cont.)*

Not sure how to spell *Renaissance?* Here it is in question 1.

---

**Example:**

1. *London* was an important city in England during the Renaissance.

2. In 1558, England defeated the *Spanish Armada* in a battle at sea.

3. Johann Gutenberg developed the *printing press* around 1450.

4. *Renaissance* is a French word meaning "rebirth."

---

## Essay

Read the question carefully.

2. Underline important instructional words that tell you how to answer the question, such as compare, contrast, explain, list, or describe.

3. Circle any vocabulary words you have studied that are in the question. You will want to give a definition of these words in your answer.

4. Now it is time to brainstorm. On the back of the test or on scratch paper, write down everything you can think of that will help you answer the question.

5. If the question is long or difficult to understand, break it down into smaller parts.

---

**Example**

Where does a cold front come from, and what kind of weather is found along this front?

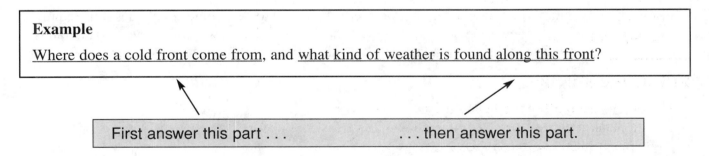

First answer this part . . .          . . . then answer this part.

---

6. Outline your ideas. Use the information from your brainstorm page, but do not feel that you have to use all of it.

7. Start your answer by restating the question.

---

**Example:**

What causes thunder? ***Thunder is caused by*** the rapid expansion of air produced by a lightning bolt. Scientists estimate . . .

---

# This Is a Test! *(cont.)*

## Essay *(cont.)*

8. Try to keep your writing simple and to the point. However, add details and examples whenever appropriate.

9. Define any vocabulary words you use in your answer.

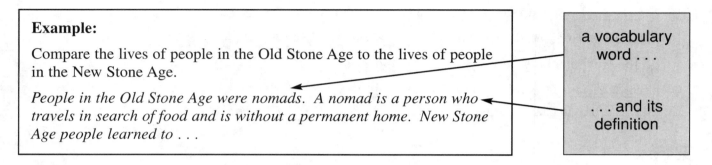

**Example:**

Compare the lives of people in the Old Stone Age to the lives of people in the New Stone Age.

*People in the Old Stone Age were nomads. A nomad is a person who travels in search of food and is without a permanent home. New Stone Age people learned to . . .*

a vocabulary word . . .

. . . and its definition

10. Proofread your answer.

   • Read through your answer slowly.

   • Be sure you have actually answered what the question is asking.

   • Check spelling and punctuation.

   • Look out for missing words. Sometimes your pencil has a hard time keeping up with your brain.

11. If you have time, add a visual to back up what you have written, such as a graph, map, time line, or drawing.

12. Be sure you know about how long your answer is expected to be. Some essay questions require an answer of only a few sentences while others may require the answer to be several paragraphs. Your teacher will probably let you know this ahead of time, but if not, **be sure to ask**.

# This Is a Test! *(cont.)*

## How to Study for Tests

Did you know that studying for a multiple choice test is very different from studying for an essay test? That's right—different types of tests require different studying methods. Once you know the difference, you can learn to prepare for tests more effectively and in less time, too.

The question types we have looked at so far in this section (matching, true/false, multiple choice, etc.) can be categorized into two different groups: *recognition* and *recall*. If you get to choose your answer, such as in multiple choice, matching, and true/false, it is a recognition question because all you have to do is recognize which answer is correct. If you have to come up with the answer on your own, such as in essay, fill-in-the-blank, and spelling tests, then it is a recall question.

**recognition question**

> Which of the following persons was a Renaissance artist?
> a. Lorenzo de' Medici
> b. Petrarch
> c. Leonardo da Vinci
> d. Martin Luther

**recall question**

> Which Renaissance artist painted the *Mona Lisa*?
>
> *Leonardo da Vinci*

## How to Study for Recognition Tests

1. Keep in mind as you study that you will be asked to recognize, or pick out, the correct answer. Therefore it will not be necessary to do a lot of memorizing, although this certainly could not hurt. Also, spelling should not be a major concern as you study since you will not be asked to spell anything that is not already printed on the test.

2. As you study, focus on names, dates, vocabulary words, and facts that seem important to the subject.

3. Make up a practice test with the types of questions you expect to see on the real test. Answer the questions on your practice test, grade it, and review the ones you missed.

4. Use the matching card method described on page 93 to study information such as facts, names, and dates.

5. Study with a partner. Have your partner ask you questions and give you several answers to choose from.

# This Is a Test! *(cont.)*

## How to Study for Recall Tests

1. As you study, focus on thorough memorization of information, including dates, facts, names, definitions, and correct spellings. If it is an essay test, focus on the definitions, examples, and general concepts of the subject you have been studying.

2. Do some brainstorming to find out how much you know about the subject. Make a list of facts, names, dates, words, definitions, details, and anything else you can think of about the subject. Do without your book at first. If your list is short and skimpy, then go back over your notes, do some re-reading from your textbook, and memorize some more information. Make a second list and compare it to the first one.

3. Use flash cards and Q & A notes to help with memorization. (See pages 78 and 71, respectively.)

4. Make a practice test with the type of questions that will be on the real test. Answer the questions on your practice test, grade it, and review the ones you missed.

5. Outlines and charts are great for essay questions. After you make an outline or chart, see if you can rewrite it from memory.

6. Try to predict what questions the teacher will ask on the test. If you were the teacher, what would you ask? What would you think the students should know? Focus on those things the teacher seemed most interested in, especially if it is a teacher-made test. Put these questions on your practice test.

## A Little of Both

Very often a test will have both recall and recognition questions. For example, a test might have 20 matching questions and two essay questions. If this is the case, try to find out from your teacher exactly how many questions of each type there will be on the test and what information they will cover. The 20 matching questions may cover vocabulary, and the two essay questions may cover the major themes of the lesson. Also, try to find out how many points each question type is worth. The matching questions may be worth one point each, while the essay questions may be worth three points each. Knowing the point value of the different question types will tell you how important the different sections of the test are in relation to each other. The more you know about the details of the test, the more you will be able to customize your studying.

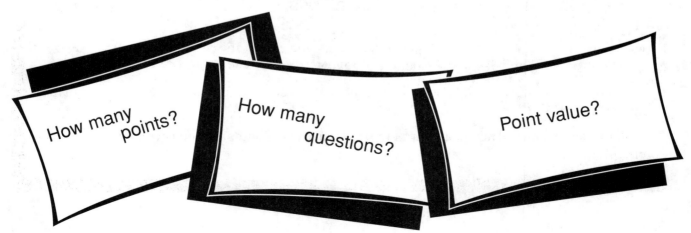

# This Is a Test! *(cont.)*

## How to Study for Open-Book and Open-Note Tests

Sometimes teachers will let you use your book to help with a test. These are called *open-book tests*. If you are allowed to use your notes, it is called an *open-note test*. Students often assume that the test will be easy because they get to look at their book or their notes. Many times students become so confident that they do not study for the open-book or open-note test at all. Never fall into that trap. An open-book test will only be easy if you prepare for it. In the paragraphs below you will find some tips for open-book and open-note tests.

## Open-Book Tests

The key to doing well on an open-book test is knowing where exactly to look in your book to find the information you need. Make a brief outline of the chapter or the part of the book you will be tested over. To make it easier to find topics in your book, add page numbers from the book to the items on your outline. Ask your teacher if you can use your outline on the test. Most importantly, be sure you have thoroughly read the entire chapter.

## Open-Note Tests

The key to doing well on open-note tests is having your notes neat and organized. If your notes are poorly written, rewrite them to make them easy to read and understand. Clean out your folder or binder and organize the papers it contains. Number the pages of your notes and make a table of contents. Your teacher may let you use other papers, such as worksheets and handouts, in addition to your notes. Be sure these papers are organized in some way, such as by subject or type. If your teacher will allow it, add extra notes to your collection. That is, write down additional information from the textbook to cover any important information that is missing from your notes.

## Taking the Open-Book or Open-Note Test

Very often on open-book or open-note tests there is not enough time to research or look up every answer. For this reason you should start the test with your book, folder, or binder closed. Answer as many questions as you can without using your book or your notes. Then go back and check answers with your book or notes. Do not spend too much time on any one question. If you cannot find the answer to a question quickly, then make a guess and go on to the next question.

# Study Tips for Math

Many of the study skills and strategies presented so far in this book are more applicable to language-based subjects than to math. In general, math relies less on language and more on numbers, formulas, and logic. Therefore, this brief chapter has been devoted solely to math. Included are general tips for solving math problems and special tips for solving word problems. A practice page for solving word problems is also provided.

## Suggested Strategies and Activities

- Practice applying the math tips with your students by having them work through sample problems which are appropriate for their level. Have the students copy the problems from the chalkboard or the overhead and have them show all of their work when solving the problems.

- If you feel it is necessary, review the multiplication tables with your students. You may want to give them a quiz to determine their competency level with these tables.

- For practice in finding careless mistakes, present your students with math problems which have been solved incorrectly because of careless mistakes. Be sure to include problems which have been solved correctly. Ask your students to determine whether or not a mistake has been made, and if so, to solve the problem correctly.

- Have your students memorize the order of operations. Students who are not using parentheses and exponents at their current math level can memorize the remaining steps.

- A practice page is provided for solving word problems (page 123). Answers are in the box below.

## Answers to Word Problems on Page 123

1. 4 brand Z batteries (2 brand X batteries last 3 hours, and 2 brand Z batteries last 9 hours.)

2. $46.35 ($49.50 for pizzas delivered, minus $3.15 spent on gas)

3. $82.44 total cost ($46 for jeans, plus $45.60 for discounted shirts, equals $91.60, minus 10%)
   $20.56 saved ($103 total cost w/o discount and coupon, minus $82.44)

# Study Tips for Math *(cont.)*

As a subject, math is unique because it deals more with numbers than with language. Let's take a look at some special study tips just for math.

1. When you are copying a problem from your book or the chalkboard, be sure to get it exactly right. Before you begin solving the problem, double check that you have copied it correctly.

2. Pay close attention to your math teacher as he or she works through problems in front of the class. Take notes on the steps he or she goes through and write down the directions.

3. If you are working on a complex problem, take it one step at a time. Double check the accuracy of each step before you go onto the next.

4. If you are having trouble with the steps of a process, such as long division, say the steps aloud.

5. Follow the order of operations when solving problems: parentheses, exponents, multiply, and divide from left to right, and add and subtract from left to right. The crazy phrase below can help you remember the order of operations.

6. Beware of careless mistakes. Double check the addition, subtraction, multiplication, and division in your work.

7. Show all your work when solving a problem. This way you will be able to check your work more thoroughly. If your answer is wrong, it will be easier to see where you have made a mistake if you have shown all your work.

8. State your answers with the necessary labels or units (&, %, meters, etc.).

9. Be sure you know the times tables. The better you are at multiplication, the easier math will be. You will save time on homework and make fewer mistakes. Use flash cards to memorize the times tables. Flash cards are explained on page 78.

10. The best way to improve your math skills is through practice. The best way to practice is to do all your homework, and on time, too. Math is the easiest subject to get behind in because the skills you learn one day are based on what you learned the day before.

## The Order of Operations

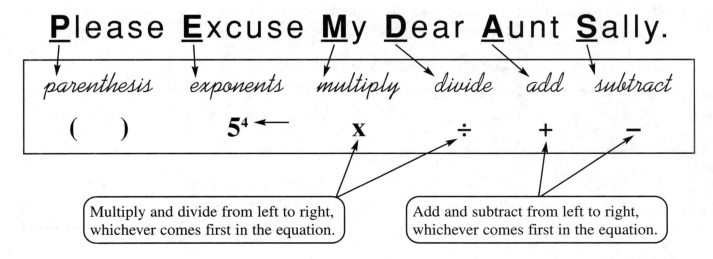

**P**lease **E**xcuse **M**y **D**ear **A**unt **S**ally.

parenthesis   exponents   multiply   divide   add   subtract

( )   $5^4$   x   ÷   +   −

Multiply and divide from left to right, whichever comes first in the equation.

Add and subtract from left to right, whichever comes first in the equation.

# Study Tips for Math *(cont.)*

## Special Tips for Word Problems

When you are solving a word problem, follow a definite procedure or set of steps such as the ones below.

1. Read the problem twice.

2. If you are allowed to write on the test, underline or circle the important parts of the problem, such as the numbers and the facts.

3. Decide what steps are required and what mathematical processes (x, ÷, +, −,) will be needed for each step. To do this you may need to reread the problem.

4. State your answer with the necessary labels or units ($, %, meters, etc.).

5. Double check your answer by rereading the problem and checking your math.

   • You may find it helpful to visualize the problem. This means seeing a picture of it in your mind.

   • You may also find it helpful to draw a picture or a diagram of the problem.

### Example

You have decided to treat your classmates to doughnuts, but you are not sure if you have enough money to buy doughnuts for the entire class. There are <u>28 students</u> in the class, including yourself, <u>and one teacher</u>. <u>Doughnuts cost $1.50</u> per dozen, <u>or 15 cents a piece</u>. How much will it cost to buy enough doughnuts so that each member of the class and your teacher <u>can have one</u>?

1. How many doughnuts will you need? (addition)

   <u>29 doughnuts needed</u> (28 students + 1 teacher = <u>29</u>)

2. How many dozen doughnuts can you buy without going over 29? (division & multiplication)

   <u>2 dozen</u> (2 x 12 = <u>24</u>)

3. How many single doughnuts will you need to buy in order to have 29 total? (subtraction)

   5 single doughnuts (29 − 24 = <u>5</u>)

4. How much will two dozen doughnuts cost? (multiplication)

   2 dozen cost $3.00 (2 x 1.50 = <u>3.00</u>)

5. How much will 5 single doughnuts cost? (multiplication)

   5 single cost $.75 (5 x .15 = <u>.75</u>)

6. What will be the total cost for purchasing 2 dozen doughnuts and 5 single doughnuts? (addition)

   <u>$3.75</u> (3.00 + .75 = <u>3.75</u>)

# Study Tips for Math *(cont.)*

## Practice: Word Problems

Solve the word problems below, using the steps from page 122.  Be sure to show all your work.

1.  Tomorrow you are leading a research team into a deep cave to do some exploring.  You expect the expedition to last 14 hours.  The last time you went caving, the two brand X batteries in your flashlight lasted only three hours.  However, the new brand Z batteries you have purchased are supposed to last three times as long as the brand X.  How many brand Z batteries will you need for tomorrow's expedition?

2.  At your job, delivering pizzas, you earn $2.75 for each delivery.  However, you must use your own car and pay for your own gas.  Gas costs 90 cents per gallon.  On one particular day you delivered 18 pizzas and used three and a half gallons of gas.  Taking into account the money you spent on gas, how much money in profit did you make that day delivering pizzas?

3.  You are purchasing two pairs of jeans and three shirts from the store, and you have a special coupon for ten percent off your entire purchase.  The regular cost for a pair of jeans is $23.00, and the regular cost for a shirt is $19.00.  However, the store is having a special sale, and all shirts are marked twenty percent off.  Using your coupon, how much will your purchase cost?  How much money did you save with the sale and your coupon?

# Using Technology

How many of your students use a computer or other forms of modern technology to complete assignments? More and more students are making use of technology, often for entertainment but also for learning. This chapter is designed to give students some ideas for using technology as an aid for school-related tasks. Although the main focus is on computers and software, uses for video and audio recordings are also presented.

Some or all of the activities below may or may not be applicable to your situation, depending on the facilities that are available to you and your students. As technology becomes more affordable, of course, accessibility will increase.

## Suggested Strategies and Activities

- Integrate technology into your classroom whenever possible. This will keep you and your students up to date on the latest technology applicable to education.

- Allow students to use a computer to complete assignments involving word processing and desktop publishing. Students can take turns and pair up to help each other. Students who are proficient with computers and software can help tutor those who are less adept.

- Have your students enter their grades from your class into an electronic database. This will give them experience working with a database, and it will keep them informed about their averages.

- Have each student keep a grade sheet such as the one described on page 45. Each student can be allotted a certain amount of time each week or so to input his or her grades into the database and print out a progress report. Customize a database file for your grading system and create a separate file for each student.

- Have your students keep a personal spelling list on paper. Allow each student to input his or her words into an electronic database. Customize a file with fields or categories such as *name, class, spelling word, date entered, date learned,* and *activities tried,* and create a file for each student. Frequently have your students update their words in the database, adding new words and changing the *learned/unlearned* status of others. To read more about personal spelling lists, see page 95.

- Have students report on software they use, its uses, strengths, and weaknesses. Share information about software you use as well.

- Beware of computer viruses. Do not allow students to load any software they have brought from home without having it scanned for viruses first.

- Allow your students to use video or audio recordings in their projects. Set minimum and maximum time limits for the length of the recording. Be sure to preview student recordings before showing them to the class. Also, to ensure that no cassette is tampered with, require that the tabs be removed from the cassette before it is submitted.

- Allow your students to practice making recordings for studying. If cassette players are few, have them work in pairs.

- Review the proper care procedures for computer disks and video and audio cassettes with your students whenever you have an activity involving these items.

# Using Technology *(cont.)*

Modern technology helps to make our lives better in many ways, even when it comes to schoolwork. In this chapter we will look at three tools modern technology has to offer that can be used for studying and completing schoolwork: computers, video recordings, and audio recordings.

## Computers: Uses for Studying

There are many different ways you can use a computer to help with studying and doing homework. First, we will look at ways to use word processing programs and database programs. Then we will focus on some special tips for using computers and computer software.

## Word Processing Programs

### Homework Assignments

Most writing assignments that you normally complete on loose-leaf paper can be created in a word processing program. Essays, reports, answers to review questions, and journal entries are just a few examples. The quick writing steps below can be used with a data processing program. To find out more about quick writing, see page 104.

1. Brainstorm ideas. Type these ideas on paper or in a text frame as you think of them.

2. Create a chart for organizing your ideas.

3. Drop or copy the ideas you decide to use from your brainstorm list to the chart. As you do this, rearrange the order of ideas so that they are better organized.

4. Use the chart as a guide for writing the assignment.

5. When you finish writing, proofread and edit the assignment. Use any spelling and grammar tools included in the program.

6. If you have time, add a graphic, such as a piece of clip art or a graph.

7. Print a hard copy of the assignment and proofread it again. Sometimes things appear slightly different on paper than they do on the monitor, such as spacing and margins.

### Rewriting Notes

Many students find it helpful to rewrite their notes. Rewriting lecture notes or reading notes can help you organize the information and make it easier to understand. You can use a word processing program to rewrite your notes.

# **Using Technology** *(cont.)*

## Database Programs

Database programs can be used to store information that you are studying. You can store facts, formulas, spelling words, vocabulary words and definitions, questions and answers, and more. Using a database makes it possible to organize and reorganize this information quickly and easily.

### Spelling Lists

You can use a database to store lists of spelling words. Each time you receive a spelling list from your teacher, enter the words into a database file. After you have a spelling test, mark any words that you missed on the test in the database file. This can be done by creating a field or category titled "missed," and placing a Y (for yes) in that field for each word that was missed on the test. Later, after you have had several spelling tests, use the program to list only the words that you have missed on those tests. To do this, have the program list only the words which are marked with a Y in the "missed" field. As you have more tests, your "missed words" list may grow longer. Study these words. Each time you learn to spell a word correctly, remove the Y from the "missed" category. This will remove the word from your missed words list. Take a look at the example below.

| Spelling List #1 | |
|---|---|
| **Word** | **Missed?** |
| necessary | |
| carefully | y |
| quiet | |
| though | |
| calendar | y |
| possess | y |
| governor | |
| absolutely | |
| ceiling | |

| Missed Words List | |
|---|---|
| **Word** | **From List #1** |
| carefully | 1 |
| calendar | 1 |
| possess | 1 |
| neighbor | 2 |
| license | 3 |
| similar | 3 |
| embarrass | 4 |
| luxury | 4 |
| permanent | 5 |

# Using Technology *(cont.)*

## Database Programs *(cont.)*

### Making Tests and Quizzes

Another use of a database program can be to create your own tests over information that you are studying. Creating and taking your own tests can help you learn the information. It can also help you find out what information you have not learned. Many database programs have special test-making features designed especially for teachers. These features make it easy to create a matching quiz or a fill-in-the-blank test. Save your "homemade test" files, and later you can easily review several chapters worth of information for a unit test or a final exam.

### Personal Spelling and Vocabulary Lists

You can create a personal spelling list in a database or a word processing program. Simply create a file and name it something like "pspellst." You can easily add and delete words on the list, or you can store several lists at a time. You can also do this for personal vocabulary lists. To find out more about personal spelling lists, see page 95. To find out more about personal vocabulary lists, see page 67.

### Reading Journals

Use a database program to store information about books you read. Each time you finish a book, make a journal entry into your database program. Include the following fields or categories: date, title of book, author, copyright date, ISBN number, type of literature, age level, subject of the story, a short summary, and your likes and dislikes about the book. After a few years, you will have a database full of information about dozens, or perhaps hundreds of different books. This can be very helpful when you are choosing a book for a report, or when you are doing research on a certain topic. You can simply go to your database and pull up information about books you have already read. Take a look at the example of a database journal entry below.

---

**Date of Journal Entry:** 11/98

**Title:** *Amazing Structure: The Great Wall of China*

**Author:** Jill Shihuangdi

**Type:** nonfiction        **Age Level:** young adult

**Copyright:** 1988        **ISBN#:** 0-09-12458-0

**Subject(s):** China, history, defensive structures, architecture

**Summary:**     This book tells the story of the building of the Great Wall, how it was constructed, and what was going on in China at the time. It has many pictures, diagrams, and maps. There are other books in this series about famous structures around the world.

**Likes/Dislikes:** Great book! The pictures are beautiful. It makes me want to visit China. I especially like the parts about Chinese history.

---

# Using Technology *(cont.)*

## Computers: Special Tips

### The Pitfalls of Spelling Check Programs

*You* are smarter than your computer. Keep this in mind when you use a program to check the spelling in your assignments. Programs that check spelling cannot proofread your work. They cannot find mistakes involving apostrophes, capitalization, plurality, usage, or syntax. The spelling check will point out only the words which are not in its dictionary and give you a list of similar words to choose from. In order to choose the correct word from the list, you will need to know its correct spelling, so keep your dictionary handy.

Use the spelling check to find as many mistakes as it can, but also be sure to proofread thoroughly. And, if your spelling check keeps finding the same words misspelled, then be sure to add those words to your personal spelling list.

---

### Mistakes That the Spelling Check Missed

The old stadium <u>hash</u> <u>ben</u> <u>their</u> <u>four</u> many years.

The essay <u>saw</u> over 500 <u>wards</u> long.

As a judge, I had to <u>chose</u> a <u>winners</u> and a <u>loser</u>.

Did you <u>sea</u> the latest James <u>bond</u> movie?

<u>Its</u> <u>to</u> bad <u>you</u> car broke down.

Many people <u>car</u> about what <u>happen</u> to <u>home</u> <u>less</u> children.

<u>Are</u> vacation to Africa <u>as</u> really <u>Exciting</u>.

---

### Saving Your Work

All of the work you do on your computer is stored electronically. Unfortunately, this means that it can be lost or erased very easily. These are just a few of the things that can cause your work to be lost: a power outage, a close lightning strike, a computer virus, a shortage in random access memory, or problems with the hard drive. Even entering the wrong command by mistake can cause hours of work to be wiped out. For this reason it is very important to save and back up your work very often. Save your work at least every twenty minutes. Back up your files daily by copying them to a floppy disk.

It is also a good idea to print a hard copy of your work often, even if you have not finished the assignment. A hard copy is a printed page or pages of your work. This is another way of backing up your work. If for some reason your file is lost or damaged, you will be able to use the hard copy to recreate the file. Also, when you print a hard copy of your work, jot down the name of the file in the corner or on the back of the paper. This will help you keep track of the file name of each assignment.

# Using Technology *(cont.)*

## Computers: Special Tips *(cont.)*

### Organizing Your Files

File names are limited in the number of characters they can have. For example, if you create a file for an essay about your winter vacation, you may not be able to name it winter vacation essay. You might have to shorten the name to something like *wvacesay,* or *essay #14,* especially if you do not use the Windows 95 software. Abbreviated file names can be a problem, though, because they do not give enough information. Later on you might not remember what some of the abbreviations stand for. For this reason, it is a good idea to keep a list of your filenames and a description of each. This will make it easier to find the file you are looking for, especially if you have not used it in a while. Take a look at the sample list of file names and descriptions below.

| Date Made | File Name | Description |
| --- | --- | --- |
| 9/10 | scriqp21 | science review questions page 21 |
| 9/13 | svacesay | essay for English about my summer vacation |
| 9/25 | molecdgm | molecule diagram for chapter 3 group project |
| 9/29 | phonelst | phone numbers of friends |
| 10/13 | bbysit#s | list of people to baby-sit for & their phone #s |

### Floppy Disk

There are two important things to remember about floppy disks—label them completely, and care for them so that they do not get damaged. Like labeling your papers, labeling your disks can save you much time in the long run, especially if you have many of them. Label the disk with your name, your school's name, and the name of your homeroom teacher. If you lose your disk, you will have a good chance of getting it back with a complete label. Whenever you add a file to a disk, write the name of the file on the disk label. This will make it easier to find that file later. Take a look at the example on the next page.

Floppy disks are easily damaged. This can cause all the information on the disk to be ruined. Keep your disks away from magnets, magnetized objects, and speakers. Avoid exposing them to temperatures below 50° F (10° C) or above 140° F (60° C). If your disk has become too hot or too cold, let it adjust to room temperature for about an hour before using it. Avoid exposing your disks to a lot of dust, direct sunlight, or moisture, either rain or high humidity. Be extra careful with disks that you take to and from school. Keep these disks in a bag or case. And most importantly, make a back up copy of each of your floppy disks, or at least the files that are most important. If one of your disks get damaged, you will still have a copy of the files on your back up disk.

# Using Technology *(cont.)*

## Video and Audio Recording

There are many uses for video and audio recording when it comes to schoolwork. A few suggestions are listed below.

1. Make a video or audio recording of a presentation of a speech you are preparing for. Play back the tape of your performance. Take notes on how you can improve your presentation, and practice it a few more times. Make another recording and critique it again. Continue practicing and recording until you get it just right.

2. Prepare a project with a video recording. Projects can include an interview, a skit, or a report on a special location or event. For example, for a project on your favorite hobby, ice skating, you could tape and show one of your competition performances.

3. As a social studies project, videotape a "newscast from history." Write a short script which includes events from the place and period you are studying in your social studies class. The script can be written so that newscasters review the top stories from that place and time in history. You can also dress in a costume from that time in history and have pictures in the background which highlight the top stories. This can also be done to review the important details from a unit or chapter. You can make a "radio" newscast with audio tape if video is not available.

4. With a very involved project, you may want to videotape some scenes of the planning and construction of it. When you present your project to the class, include a short (5 minute) video presentation of "the making of" your project.

5. As a unique way to study vocabulary, videotape yourself acting out the meaning of each word. Invite a few friends over, watch the video, and have a good laugh reviewing the meanings of the words.

6. Video tape yourself taking a practice spelling test. Write large letters with a marker so you will be able to see each word on the recording. To grade the test, play back the video and watch yourself, checking your spelling with an answer key. Watching and grading your own mistakes may help you spell the words correctly.

7. Science teachers sometimes assign simple lab experiments at home. When doing such labs, you can videotape the steps of the experiment and the results. Of course, any written part of the assignment, such as your hypothesis, observations, and conclusions, should be turned in along with the video.

8. To be sure your video or audio recording is not erased or recorded over, remove the tab or tabs from the cassette. If later you want to record on the cassette again, simply cover each hole with cellophane tape.

9. Avoid exposing your cassettes to dust, direct sunlight, or moisture. Avoid exposing them to temperatures below 50° F (10° C) or above 140° F (60° C). If your cassette has become too hot or too cold, let it adjust to room temperature for about an hour before using it. Be extra careful with cassettes that you take to and from school. Keep these cassettes in a bag or case.

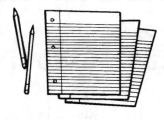
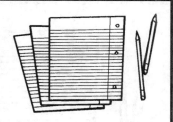

# Class Supply List

Use this form to list the supplies you'll need at the beginning of the year for each class.
Then use the Supply Master List form to list the combined supplies for all of your classes.

| Math | Science |
|------|---------|
| | |

| Language Arts | Social Studies |
|---------------|----------------|
| | |

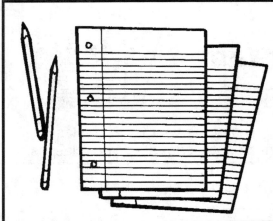

# Supply Master List

Use this form to list the combined supplies for all of your classes at the beginning of the year. Be sure to take this list with you to the store.

| | supply type | quantity | special | have it ✔ | notes |
|---|---|---|---|---|---|
| 1. | loose-leaf paper | | | | |
| 2. | folder | | | | |
| 3. | spiral notebook | | | | |
| 4. | binder | | | | |
| 5. | No. 2 pencils | | | | |
| 6. | colored pencils | | | | |
| 7. | pens | | | | |
| 8. | markers | | | | |
| 9. | crayons | | | | |
| 10. | ruler | | | | |
| 11. | pencil sharpener, hand held | | | | |
| 12. | pencil box/case | | | | |
| 13. | index cards | | | | |
| 14. | book covers | | | | |
| 15. | poster board | | | | |
| 16. | construction paper | | | | |
| 17. | tape | | | | |
| 18. | scissors | | | | |
| 19. | stapler and/or staples | | | | |
| 20. | hole puncher | | | | |
| 21. | electric pencil sharpener | | | | |
| 22. | book bag | | | | |
| 23. | calculator | | | | |
| 24. | P.E. clothes | | | | |
| 25. | other: | | | | |
| 26. | other: | | | | |
| 27. | other: | | | | |

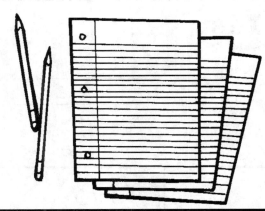

# Supply Update List

Keep a copy of this form in your home folder and take it with you to each class. When a teacher mentions a supply you will need, or when you find that you are running low on something, write it down.

| today's date | Supply Type | date needed |
|---|---|---|
| | | |

notes:

# Homework List

Name _____

Date _____

| priority order | class | assignment | M T W Th F notes |
|---|---|---|---|
|  | _____ |  |  |
|  | _____ |  |  |
|  | _____ |  |  |
|  | _____ |  |  |
|  | _____ |  |  |

# Assignment Sheet

Name _____

Date _____

M T W Th F

| today's class | tonight's homework | priority order | finished |
|---|---|---|---|
| class_____<br>conduct _____<br>homework _____<br>teacher<br>signature _____ | | | |
| class_____<br>conduct _____<br>homework _____<br>teacher<br>signature _____ | | | |
| class_____<br>conduct _____<br>homework _____<br>teacher<br>signature _____ | | | |
| class_____<br>conduct _____<br>homework _____<br>teacher<br>signature _____ | | | |
| class_____<br>conduct _____<br>homework _____<br>teacher<br>signature _____ | | | |

parent signature_____ date _____

comments:

# Daily Schedule

Name _____

## Time    Activity

morning

_____ to _____    <u>Wake up/get ready for school</u>

_____ to _____    _____

_____ to _____    _____

_____ to _____    <u>School</u>

afternoon

_____ to _____    _____

_____ to _____    _____

_____ to _____    _____

_____ to _____    _____

_____ to _____    _____

_____ to _____    _____

_____ to _____    <u>to bed</u>

study session _____

fun _____

sleep_____

notes

**Month:** _____

**Year:** _____

| Sun | Mon | Tue | Wed | Thu | Fri | Sat |
|-----|-----|-----|-----|-----|-----|-----|
|     |     |     |     |     |     |     |
|     |     |     |     |     |     |     |
|     |     |     |     |     |     |     |
|     |     |     |     |     |     |     |
|     |     |     |     |     |     |     |

# Grade Sheet for Points

Name _____

Class _____

Grading period _____

| Date | Assignment Title | Your Total Points | Total Points Possible | % Grade |
|------|------------------|-------------------|----------------------|---------|
|      |                  |                   |                      |         |
|      |                  |                   |                      |         |
|      |                  |                   |                      |         |
|      |                  |                   |                      |         |
|      |                  |                   |                      |         |
|      |                  |                   |                      |         |
|      |                  |                   |                      |         |
|      |                  |                   |                      |         |
|      |                  |                   |                      |         |
|      |                  |                   |                      |         |
|      |                  |                   |                      |         |
|      |                  |                   |                      |         |
|      |                  |                   |                      |         |
|      |                  |                   |                      |         |
|      |                  |                   |                      |         |
|      |                  |                   |                      |         |
|      |                  |                   |                      |         |
|      |                  |                   |                      |         |

| Date | Assignment Title | Your Total Points | Total Points Possible | % Grade |
|------|------------------|-------------------|-----------------------|---------|
|      |                  |                   |                       |         |
|      |                  |                   |                       |         |
|      |                  |                   |                       |         |
|      |                  |                   |                       |         |
|      |                  |                   |                       |         |
|      |                  |                   |                       |         |
|      |                  |                   |                       |         |
| **Totals ➡** |          |                   |                       |         |

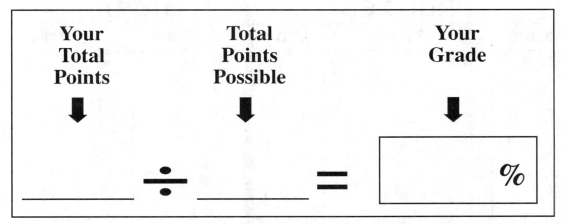

To figure out your grade, divide your **total points** by the **total points possible**. The answer will have a decimal. Remove the decimal and add a percent. That number is your grade. Fill in the grading scale and see what your letter grade is.

## Grading Scale

**A** from _____ to _____ %

**B** from _____ to _____ %

**C** from _____ to _____ %

**D** from _____ to _____ %

**F** below _____ %

# Grade Sheet

### for percentages

Name_____

Date_____

Grading period_____

## Tests

| Date | Title | Grade |
|------|-------|-------|
|      |       |       |
|      |       |       |
|      |       |       |

Total_____

Average = total ÷ number of grades

**My test average is_____.**

## Projects

| Date | Title | Grade |
|------|-------|-------|
|      |       |       |
|      |       |       |
|      |       |       |

Total_____

**My project average is_____.**

## Quizzes

| Date | Title | Grade |
|------|-------|-------|
|      |       |       |
|      |       |       |
|      |       |       |

Total_____

**My quiz average is_____.**

## Other:

| Date | Title | Grade |
|------|-------|-------|
|      |       |       |
|      |       |       |
|      |       |       |

Total_____

**My average in this category is_____.**

### Other:

| Date | Title | Grade |
|------|-------|-------|
|      |       |       |

Total_____

**My average in this category is_____.**

### Other:

| Date | Title | Grade |
|------|-------|-------|
|      |       |       |

Total_____

**My average in this category is_____.**

| Grade Weightings (from the teacher) | multiply | decimal | your category average | total in each category |
|---|---|---|---|---|
| tests . . . . . . . . . . _____% | *times (x)* | • | _____ = _____ | |
| quizzes. . . . . . . . _____% | *times (x)* | • | _____ = _____ | |
| projects . . . . . . . _____% | *times (x)* | • | _____ = _____ | |
| other:_____ . . _____% | *times (x)* | • | _____ = _____ | |
| other:_____ . . _____% | *times (x)* | • | _____ = _____ | |
| other:_____ . . _____% | *times (x)* | • | _____ = _____ | |
| other:_____ . . _____% | *times (x)* | • | _____ = _____ | |

**total grade** _____ %

To figure out your grade, follow the six steps below.

1. Write in the grade weightings that your teacher uses.
2. Write in your category averages from the other side of the page (such as test average).
3. Multiply each grade weighting number times your category average. (Add a decimal in front of the category average number before you multiply. If your category average is 100, multiply the grade weighting number by 1.)
4. Put each answer in the last column, and add them all together to get your total grade.
5. Fill in the grading scale and see what your letter grade is.
6. See page 49 for an example.

## Grading Scale

**A** from _____ to _____ %

**B** from _____ to _____ %

**C** from _____ to _____ %

**D** from _____ to _____ %

**F** below _____ %

# Personal Vocabulary List

Name _____

Date _____

| Word | Your Definition | Dictionary Definition |
|------|-----------------|------------------------|
| 1. |  |  |
| 2. |  |  |
| 3. |  |  |
| 4. |  |  |
| 5. |  |  |
| 6. |  |  |
| 7. |  |  |
| 8. |  |  |
| 9. |  |  |
| 10. |  |  |

# Personal Spelling List

Use this form to keep track of words that you tend to misspell. Study the words on your list a little bit each day. When you have mastered a word, check it off your list.

| ✔ Check | Words | ✔ Check | Words |
|---------|-------|---------|-------|
| ☐ | 1. _____ | ☐ | 11. _____ |
| ☐ | 2. _____ | ☐ | 12. _____ |
| ☐ | 3. _____ | ☐ | 13. _____ |
| ☐ | 4. _____ | ☐ | 14. _____ |
| ☐ | 5. _____ | ☐ | 15. _____ |
| ☐ | 6. _____ | ☐ | 16. _____ |
| ☐ | 7. _____ | ☐ | 17. _____ |
| ☐ | 8. _____ | ☐ | 18. _____ |
| ☐ | 9. _____ | ☐ | 19. _____ |
| ☐ | 10. _____ | ☐ | 20. _____ |

# **Project Information and Planning Sheet**

| Name: | Class: |
|---|---|
| Project title: | Due date: |

Summary of project:

❑ Individual project  ❑ Group project    Group members

Materials needed:

_____

_____

_____

_____

_____

❑ Step 1

❑ Step 4

❑ Step 2

❑ Step 5

❑ Step 3

❑ Step 6